DEBORAH:
A Wilderness Narrative

DAVID ROBERTS
Author of "The Mountain of My Fear"

THE VANGUARD PRESS, INC.
NEW YORK

Photographs courtesy of Bradford Washburn (1–4), David Roberts (Title Page, 5–13), and Don Jensen (14–15).

Illustrations

7. The camp on the col, looking north, before the storms hit.

8. Jensen at the top of the second pitch (rotten rock) on the east ridge.

9. On the east ridge. Looking back, one can see the col camp and climbers' tracks leading across the knife-edged ridge toward the first cliffs (Jensen seconding).

10. Jensen leading a steep traverse in the hollow snow of the east ridge.

11. Jensen seconding on the east ridge below a detached cornice. In the background, crevasses on the Gillam Glacier.

12. Jensen seconding on the most dangerous part of the climb.

13. Jensen eating lunch before the backdrop of the east ridge, on the ascent of South Hess.

14. Looking sideways (south) from the east ridge across the 5000-foot-high east face.

15. Roberts wading the East Fork of the Susitna, at the point at which the climbers finally found a crossing.

MAPS (*by John Leinung*)

Preface

This book deals with an experience I have been trying to write about, explicitly or implicitly, for the last four years, an experience that left me with so many contradictory and unfocused emotions that it has always loomed in my memory like a waking dream, edged with touches of nightmare. The experience was a mountaineering expedition, undertaken by my best friend and me in the summer of 1964, to the unexplored eastern side of Mount Deborah, in Alaska (the most beautiful mountain either of us had ever seen). It was so private an adventure that its documentation lies only in our very fallible memories, in two diaries that strangely disagree, and in the aging strands of rope and the metal spikes we left attached to the mountain. It was a journey on foot, with our food and shelter on our backs, into an undiscovered country, from which we planned to return within two months; but I have never been sure what we did discover there, if anything— or, indeed, even what we sought, beyond the mountain's summit.

One can describe such an expedition most easily in terms of camps and crevasses, pitches and pitons, sunsets and storms; but to do so is to be blind to what was going on. Closer to our hearts was an inward journey, which began with the world all before us and seemed to end in stale corridors, facing blank walls.

At the end of the trip, I was most grateful for the chance to relax, to forget about it. But within a few weeks I was trying to remember it all again. I have never since been able to recall the expedition without intense feelings, and they have been both the source of my desire to talk and write about it and the source of my difficulties in doing so. Out of the experience came several melodramatic short stories, several bad poems, several factual articles for mountaineering journals, many rhapsodic slide shows, and too many moments of nostalgia—the maudlin sort of nostalgia that takes the form of blind loyalty to the event for its own sake, so that I could even feel nostalgic for its worst moments. Hence in my imaginative writing about the expedition, I tried to reproduce this sense of loyalty by pretending that our journey had some intrinsic moral goodness about it, or that our climbing was heroic, not merely self-indulgent. These were really attempts, I think, to project meaning and justification onto an experience that still bewildered me. Of course, they failed.

In this book, then, I have tried to tell only exactly what happened. That is enough, and hard enough; it is so easy, not only at the time, but in retrospect, to dwell upon the merely circumstantial and to ignore the quietly important. It is so easy to neglect the human in favor of the scenic. As obvious as it seems, it took me a long while to realize that what had happened to us was more important than what had happened to the mountain. For, both then and later, what took place within our tent seemed so evanescent compared to what took place outside it: I could not even be sure, for instance, that, at a given moment, my vague malaise really existed—but there was no denying the violent storm that shook the tent.

In writing about it, therefore, I have tried to present our experience unemotionally, in a plain prose style perhaps appropriate to that desire. I have tried to resist the urge to make the style reflect the experience, because to do so often corrupts the experience, or results in a mannerism, an external attitude forced on the events themselves. I feel that our "accomplishments" have no interest (except to mountaineers) outside of the reader's potential interest in us, as characters, and in what went on, during this strange trip, between us. The hardest part of the writing for me was to tell objectively just what it *was* that went on between us; hence, I try to avoid being much more introspective about either of us than I was at the time, hoping that we may reveal ourselves better through the ways we acted than through what I can say about them.

DEBORAH:

A WILDERNESS NARRATIVE

1 ▲

I first met Don Jensen at the beginning of our sophomore year at Harvard. We had both joined the mountaineering club our freshman year, but had never gone
on the same week-end trip until the first rock-climbing
outing in October, 1962. I had heard of Don—other
members of the club had told me what a strong, enthusiastic climber he was. But it was something of a surprise to meet him. That Friday afternoon, I had lugged
my gear over to the entry of Lowell House, where the
cars would pick us up. With the other beginners, I
stood for a few moments in an awkward silence. Then

one of them stepped aggressively toward me, stretching out an eager hand: "Hi! I'm Don Jensen."

I shook hands and introduced myself. I was surprised because he seemed so boyishly friendly. I had imagined some cool, hard athlete. I could see that Don was powerful, about my height but much heavier, built like a football player. His black hair and solid face were strong and masculine. But his face was also young, and terribly sincere. I was used to the Harvard "style," in which one affects a biting wit and a cold heart; instead, Don reminded me of friends in Colorado, where I had grown up. We talked about climbing for a while. He was from California; as he talked, I could see that already, three weeks into the term, he was nostalgic for the Sierra Nevada. He told me about a twenty-day trip he had taken alone, following the divide southward. I had never been out for that long, let alone by myself; I suggested that he must have got lonely. On the contrary, he had found the several people he had run into a disappointment. Once he had seen a large group of Sierra Club hikers, and had deliberately skirted them so that he would not have to talk to them.

Don and I both lived in Dunster House, so that fall we saw each other often. We ate lunch and dinner together frequently, talking about little else than climbing. It was, for each of us, the primary pleasure in life. I was majoring in mathematics, with vague plans of a career in research and teaching. Don, with the same vague plans, was struggling with philosophy. But in our spare time I dreamed about the Rockies, Don about the

Sierras. A dozen times I went up to Don's room, to find maps spread on the floor, the corners held down with Kant and Wittgenstein and Aristotle. And whenever Don came up to my room, I insisted on hauling out my muddy three-by-five snapshots of Colorado peaks.

With another friend, we planned a Christmas trip climbing in the Crestones, in southern Colorado. Don flew home for Christmas, then back to Denver, where I met him at the airport. I had never seen him in such good spirits. He didn't really like the East; this land of unlimited sky and sun—anywhere from Nebraska to Oregon—was his spiritual habitat.

The three of us had a fine six-day trip, the longest I had ever taken in the winter. The weather was perfect each day. We camped on the frozen bed of a river at 12,000 feet, crowded snugly into a three-man tent we had rented. We found running water by chopping through the ice. It got bitterly cold each night (perhaps twenty below), but we were up before dawn to get a good start on the peaks. We climbed two of them, both over 14,000 feet, and had to stop short of the summit of a third when our friend got sick. On the sixth day we hiked back out to our car. It was a wonderfully happy trip, and we dreaded going back to Harvard. For the first time, I think, I felt an alliance with Don that went beyond friendship: we began to feel the cooperative excitement of a good team. But I also noticed, for the first time, two things that would cause trouble between us later: often, at night, we ran out of things to talk about; in addition, I loved conversations but Don preferred to think by himself. The other disparity had to do with a kind of emotional endurance: at the end of the six days I felt satisfied, without much desire to climb any more right away; but Don saw peaks and ridges surrounding our camp that we hadn't had time to climb, and he felt as if he had cheated himself by not arranging for at least a few more days there. Don could never see a mountain, even an ugly mountain or an easy one, without feeling a duty to climb it. Instead, I chose the ones I was most interested in and tended to ignore the rest.

Back at school, we faced papers and finals. I managed to get through them but Don procrastinated on his papers and began to panic; he took NōDōz to stay awake but couldn't concentrate. He began to look rundown: he gained weight, and his tough, youthful face grew haggard. At last he got everything finished but he knew he had done badly. What was worse, he saw how much of a drain on his health school could be; with the attitude of any true outdoorsman, Don valued his physical well-being above his mental achievements.

He began the spring semester of 1963 with a determination to do better. But everything went badly from the start. More and more he turned to his maps and thoughts of the stark, splendid mountains of California. He had never spent much time in them in the winter; our Christmas trip had obviously sown the seeds of restlessness. Moreover, in February I was invited by the older, more experienced members of the mountaineering club to go on an expedition to Mount

McKinley, in Alaska; I felt extremely flattered, because
the others had climbed all over the western United
States, and in the Canadian Rockies and Coast Range;
one had even been on McKinley before. Don, though,
was not invited. It seemed unfair to me, because we
were equally skillful; if anything, Don had more experience on snow. But I was also selfishly pleased to be the
only sophomore chosen. Don generously claimed that
he was glad for my sake and that being left out made
little difference to him; but his disappointment was evident.

Shortly after that, he decided to drop out of school
for the semester. I was surprised and tried to joke him
out of it. But he had carefully made up his mind before
telling anyone. He was going to go home—not to his
parents' house near San Francisco but to the little town
of Big Pine, on the eastern slope of the Sierras. I knew
this was only a few miles from his favorite mountains,
the Palisades, so I kidded him about being a hedonist.
But he had a perfect rationalization: he was planning
to take Professor Riesman's course on social structures
in America when he returned the next fall; hence he
would do field research on the natives of Big Pine. He
described the complicated web of cliques and prejudices
he had noticed there before. I tried to picture Don,
camped just outside town all spring in the little orange
tent he had just made for himself, sneaking in during
the day to interview old ladies. But he could not be
joked out of it; he had made up his mind.

He had almost run out of money. He stopped going

to classes but he could not pull himself together and actually leave. I think he was a little afraid that he was letting his parents down and, with them, all the high-school friends who had expected so much of him when he first went to Harvard. He stopped eating, for the most part, to save money; for about a week he staggered about in a ravenous daze. At last he was kicked out of his room in Dunster House, so he moved to the mountaineering clubroom, a damp closet in the basement of Lowell House. I felt sorry for him, but he was so ludicrous that I couldn't help laughing at him. I would sneak bread and rolls out of the dining hall for him; one evening I smuggled him into a beer-and-sandwiches reception with the master. Having shipped most of his clothes home, he had to go to the reception wearing a dirty shirt, a borrowed coat, grass-stained Levis, and his climbing boots. The master was surprised to see him at all, and especially in such a state, but he maintained decorum. The master's wife nervously watched as Don wolfed down sandwich after sandwich.

The day before he left, I bought some bread and cheese and we had a picnic in a Cambridge park. We called the little lunch the "Don C. Jensen Memorial Farewell Dinner." For once during these last few weeks, Don was in fine humor; we laughed at every remark, releasing tensions and covering the genuine sadness we felt at saying good-by to each other. There was a warm, wet breeze; it seemed the first day of spring. We promised each other all sorts of climbs together in the vague future. After the picnic, I saw Don to the bus depot.

He wrote me one or two letters from Big Pine. Needless to say, he was spending every moment in the Palisades, descending to town only to get food. In rapturous terms he described holding down his tent, alone, during a week-long blizzard that had threatened to tear it loose. He was reading Goethe, he said, and learning more than he ever could have in school. He described a natural echoing rock he had discovered; in good weather he would go out and shout to it for hours on end, carrying on eloquent conversations with it.

That spring I was preoccupied with planning for McKinley. We were going to attempt its Wickersham Wall, or north face, by a rather audacious route straight up the middle of it. This was the last side of McKinley that no one had climbed, and the Wall was one of the two or three biggest cliffs in the world, rising more than 14,000 vertical feet from bottom to top. I had never even seen such a mountain. Privately, I felt sure we were too ambitious and I anticipated the summer with a kind of fear. But I didn't show the others my reluctance and the more I got involved in the work, the more enthusiastic I grew. At the Spring Dinner meeting, I was elected the club's vice-president.

Then, a few weeks before we were to start for Alaska, one of the expedition's six members dropped out. We frantically looked around for another experienced climber who could go on such short notice. I urged the others to ask Don. None of them knew Don well; one of them had scarcely met him. But as I described Don's talents, they were gradually won over.

The next problem was to contact Don. We quickly found out that he had last been seen trudging back into the Palisades. We felt frustrated; in desperation we sent a telegram to General Delivery in Big Pine. A few days later Don happened to come out for supplies and got the telegram. At once he called us, agreeing to go. In a matter of days he got together all the gear he would need and arranged a ride to Alaska. We would meet him in McKinley Park.

School let out in June. We packed supplies nonstop at a friend's house in New York, then drove nonstop to Alaska, over the forty-eight hundred miles of dreary road. Six days later we arrived at the little railroad stop of McKinley Park (a full hundred miles away from the mountain) in a dismal rain; that afternoon Don showed up, soaking wet, from a three-day climb he had gone on while waiting for us. I was especially glad to see him. He looked so much healthier than when he had left Harvard that I could hardly believe only two months had gone by.

The expedition went smoothly. In thirty-five days we hiked in to the Peters Glacier, climbed our route without a serious mishap, traversed over the mountain, climbed both its summits, descended the easy route, and hiked out. Unknown to us, we had caused a national scare for a few days in July, when we were reported missing. Of course we didn't know we were "missing"; we had simply been ahead of schedule. It had been a difficult climb and a tiring trip, and we were all glad to get back; but the adventure had been closer to a lark than an ordeal. There were enough of us so that we never grew lonely and so that no personal antagonisms built up too high. At times some of us got angry at one another, but it never lasted.

Don and I had not climbed together very much on the expedition because the older members wisely insisted on splitting up, so that one of them always climbed with one of us. On the few occasions when Don and I shared a rope, I noticed the return of the "team" feeling we had discovered in Colorado, a feeling I hadn't developed with any of the others. On the last stretch of the hike out, Don and I had roped together to cross the McKinley River; both of us, I think, felt that that was fitting to our sense of comradeship.

In the fall of 1963, Don was back at Harvard. He had been moved from Dunster House to Claverly, the overflow hall, which was the least popular place to live. I first saw him that September carrying his refrigerator out of Dunster House. He put it down and we shook hands, much differently than we had the first time. We both felt proud of our summer; in fact, most of our friends at Harvard had heard about our climb and had congratulated us the first moment they saw us.

Don and I climbed together often during the fall weekends. We played touch football in the afternoons and sometimes worked out together, running a circuit of bridges over the Charles River or exercising in the fieldhouse. We planned another Christmas trip to

Colorado; at first it was designed as a six- or seven-day trip, like the one before, but Don talked me into using every minute of our vacation that we could, even Christmas and New Year's Day. By driving straight through to Colorado and back, we could arrange an eleven-day trip.

By now Don was treasurer of the club and I was vice-president. Most of the veteran members, our McKinley friends, had graduated. So Don and I talked four of the less experienced club members into going with us. We were planning to visit the Needle Mountains, near Durango, in southwestern Colorado. No one had ever been there in the winter.

At last Christmas came. The six of us managed to get out to my home in Boulder, where we packed supplies frantically all night. In the morning the other four drove to Silverton, while Don and I flew to Durango. From the air we could see our mountains, gleaming with new snow. We hitchhiked from Durango to Silverton. It was a warm winter day and the blazing sun and dry air exhilarated us. We talked about the other four and agreed that we would have to split up, just as our more experienced friends on McKinley had split up to climb with us.

We met the others after dark in a bar in Silverton. That night we camped outside town. It got very cold, but the morning was clear and warm. We set off down the snow-covered railroad tracks, all of us excited, two days before Christmas. But it took three days, through bad brush and occasionally deep snow, to reach our mountains. Don and I watched, a little nervously, for signs of discouragement among the others: the signs were there. In the next two days we climbed three different peaks among the six of us. But already some of the others were getting edgy; the youngest and least experienced of them, a sophomore named Matt Hale, was apparently altitude-sick, for he could eat almost nothing.

The sixth day dawned on a windy blizzard. We had planned to move camp that day, but only Don and I felt like going out in the storm. At last he and I decided to go ahead, leaving the others to follow the next day. As the weather improved, Don and I stopped on the top of the pass leading to the new basin. We felt a little guilty for deserting the others; but we felt a wonderful freedom to be able to climb together again without worrying about anyone else. As it turned out, two of the others hiked out the next day, fed up with the climbing. The other two, including Matt, who was genuinely sick, climbed over the pass to catch up with Don and me. But they had to stop at nightfall, exhausted, short of our camp. The next day they too decided to hike out, since there wasn't time left to accomplish anything by joining us.

So for the last five days Don and I saw no one else. This worried us, but on the third day we spotted tracks among the trees in the valley far below us and guessed that the others had hiked on out. During those first three days we made three superb climbs, one a first ascent. The weather held good and we used every available moment of the daylight. We slept soundly through the long, cold nights; when we had to hike out at last we were very sad that our perfect days had to end; that, once again, Harvard and finals were all we had to look forward to. On the three climbs we had adapted our styles of climbing to each other in nearly perfect synchronization. We had begun to feel the instinctive awareness of each other's movements, even when out of sight, and the confidence in each other that can make roped climbing one of the most sensitive means of communication.

We hiked back up the railroad tracks on the eleventh day and arrived in Silverton around noon. There we met four irritable and depressed climbers. Only Matt, who was still sick and unable to eat much, offered us any congratulations on the climbs we had done. Again Don and I felt guilty, but as we separated from the others to go back to Durango, we felt relieved for the second time to get away from the atmosphere of discouragement that surrounded them. Flying back to Denver that night, Don and I could glimpse the white mountains under a pale moon. We were tired and happy. After a while, Don fell asleep. I sat in the dark, staring out of the window of the plane, full of a wonderful feeling of companionship. This was only the beginning, I thought. We were a great team; no mountain could stop us. And somewhere out there in the dark, beyond the hills of Colorado, beyond thousands of miles of prairie and forest, was Alaska . . . .

2 ▲

When we got back, Don went through the same experience with finals that he had the year before. If anything, it was worse this time. We were both planning to go on the club's annual four-day trip in the White Mountains of New Hampshire during term break; but on the day before we were to go, the day of his last final, Don got sick. He looked terrible. We persuaded him to go to the infirmary. When a doctor took his temperature, it came out 94°. The doctor told Don, "Either this thermomenter's broken or you're dead."

So Don spent the break in bed. He recovered quickly

and the doctors never did decide what had made him sick. The spring semester of 1964 began; for a month there was little pressure and Don was able to relax somewhat. But he'd missed his last final when he got sick and had to make it up in April. The burden of it hung over him and he began to dread it out of all proportion to its importance. He remembered the year before; events seemed to be repeating the same pattern. But he thought that if he quit again he would never be allowed to finish at Harvard, so he doggedly tried to stick it out.

Meanwhile, Don and I had decided to organize an expedition for the following summer. In the spring, some older club members invited us to join them on a rather casual summer trip to the Andes. We looked over maps and pictures with them, discussed finances, and went home to talk it over with each other. After a while we agreed to turn down the invitation; we wanted something tougher, and we wanted to plan it by ourselves.

Besides, our finances pretty much restricted us to North America. The obvious choice was somewhere in Alaska again. Don and I spent long evenings in the clubroom, poring over journals, searching for pictures of Alaskan mountains. Tentatively we considered Mount St. Elias and Mount Foraker, both giants like McKinley. But we weren't enthusiastic about either. One evening I came upon a picture of Mount Deborah, a mountain in the Hayes Range we had both vaguely heard of. The picture was spectacular; an apparently sheer face swept from a pointed summit down to a broad, banded glacier. On either side were knife-sharp ridges, studded with ice flutings and seamed with dark rock. "Don, look at this!" I said.

We quickly read the article, which described the first ascent of Deborah, in 1954, by three famous mountaineers, one of whom had been on the legendary first ascent of the Eigerwand, in the Alps, way back in 1938. With growing excitement we realized that none of the parts of the mountain visible in the picture had been touched: the trio had attacked the only "reasonable" side of Deborah, out of sight to the west. Even so, they had found it an exacting climb. The article said, "It was our unanimous conclusion that Deborah was the most sensational ice climb any of us had ever undertaken."

Almost at that moment we decided on Deborah for our expedition. We argued for a few minutes about the route to try. I liked the northwest ridge; Don was intrigued by the east ridge. After a while we agreed on Don's choice, partly because it was on the exact opposite side from the route of the first ascent. It did not matter much to us that Deborah had been climbed; for all practical purposes, we would be climbing an entirely new mountain. It didn't take long to verify that no other attempts, except the first ascent, had ever been made on Deborah; that, in fact, virtually no one had been anywhere between Deborah and the gigantic Mount Hayes, twenty miles to the east. This would obviously be a very difficult climb, probably harder than the Wickersham Wall; but this was what we wanted.

We ordered the maps of the area and planned our schedule. It looked as if we could walk in from the Denali Highway, a dirt road forty miles to the south. And Deborah was surrounded by lesser mountains, only one of which had been climbed. If we could arrange enough time, we could climb peaks all over the range, perhaps even Mount Hayes itself, as well as Deborah.

The next thought was the make-up of the party. We had hoped some of the younger club members would be ready for such an expedition; but our Christmas climb made us dubious. Matt Hale had seemed the only one with the right spirit, but the altitude had made him quite sick and he had never climbed beyond the eastern United States before the Christmas trip. The Hayes Range would be no place to get sick or to lose enthusiasm. Somewhat reluctantly, we decided not to ask Matt.

We were hesitant about inviting someone we didn't know. The rest of our McKinley friends had other plans or jobs. Finally we wrote a letter to an outstanding older climber who had been recommended to us. He wrote back to say that he would be in Boston soon and would like to talk with us. When he came, Don and I tried to share our enthusiasm about Deborah with him. He looked at the maps and pictures for a very long time, without saying anything. Don and I felt awkward and wondered if the man thought we were too rash. He made, in fact, a remark to the effect that this kind of climb had not yet been done in Alaska; but we couldn't

tell whether it was in approval or chastisement. At last
he left, saying he would have to think it over. A few
weeks later he sent a postcard indicating he had decided not to go with us.

Don and I felt let down. We had almost begun to
count on the extra member. Listlessly, we talked over
other choices and reconsidered Matt. Time was growing short. Above all, we didn't want to go with someone
with whom we might not get along well, or with someone who would not be able to keep up his drive for a
long period of time.

One day Don said, "Dave, I've been thinking this
over." He paused, characteristically, to ensure my attention. "What do you think of just the two of us—a
two-man expedition?"

I was surprised. But I felt an immediate impulse in
favor of the idea, and I suppose the impulse was, in the
long run, the basis on which I decided. We both knew
that it went against all the rules. But so, in a sense, did
the route itself. With contagious enthusiasm, Don
began to list the advantages. It would make the expedition truly our own; we would do all the climbing, all of
the load-hauling, make all the decisions, and succeed or
fail on our own efforts alone. Don and I remembered
the frustration of having to carry loads over previous
sections of the route on McKinley while someone else
was exploring above. True, if we had an accident on
Deborah, we could be in serious trouble; but with only
two of us, there was less chance of an accident. We
could rent a radio to give ourselves an added safety

factor. It would be lonely—but it would be so beautiful, so truly adventurous. Finally, of course, it would mean we could stop worrying about finding a third and fourth member.

So we decided; and once we had, we never wavered. Our friends and the older club members were all skeptical; some even told us we were foolhardy. We tried to be polite and explain our reasons, most of which were, after all, rationalizations. Back of all our other feelings, we had developed a sense of common purpose that told us this was what we owed each other, that a two-man expedition was the only "right" expression for our partnership. We had got along so well at Christmas, after we had escaped from the others. Deborah would be like that, we guessed—longer and more trying, of course, but essentially amicable.

Yet even as we decided, we began to notice the weaknesses in our friendship. Don was feeling more and more oppressed by school; every paper was an agony, and he could scarcely concentrate. In addition, he complained often to me, in somewhat paranoid terms, about his problems. I found "getting through" easy, so I tended to be unsympathetic; the more Don complained, the more irritated I grew. I realized that I had never been sympathetic to this problem of Don's; but the year before, I had been able to laugh at it; this year I couldn't. Don transferred his feelings about everything connected with Harvard to New England itself. He claimed that people in the West were basically friendlier and more human. I began to develop a real hostility toward his feelings, because I liked Harvard and the East. So instead of listening, I would argue with Don, trying to show him how ridiculous his ideas were; and, when that failed, I would cruelly make fun of them. Whatever the cause really was, Don was certainly unhappy, and his physical condition suffered with his mental one.

At the same time, Don threw himself into planning for Deborah. He studied maps for hours, made a catalogue of the whole range, and made a careful drawing of the east ridge of Deborah in elaborate detail. I lacked the patience for such tedium. I preferred to spend most of my free time playing tennis or baseball, or dating, or climbing on the weekends. Don actually stayed home from several weekend climbing trips in order to plan for Deborah. He began visibly to resent my unconcern. I claimed, in defense, that he planned so elaborately only to escape studying; there was a germ of truth in this, but it was an ungenerous remark.

We came to a temporary impasse on the question of how much time to devote to Deborah. I thought twenty days would be enough; Don was sure that would be inadequate. He would have liked to spend the whole summer in the Hayes Range. I remembered how anxious I had been to get back after a month on McKinley, and doubted that I could enjoy the Hayes Range for a whole summer. At last we compromised on two months, with seventy-two days' food, allowing a margin. We would airdrop forty-four days' food below Deborah, the other twenty-eight days' worth in a high basin just west of Mount Hayes. Since we would not pick up the second airdrop until after we had used up the first, there was a good chance the second might be buried by the snows of the intervening weeks. But we could think of no alternative.

Most of this planning was Don's; I let him figure out the details, then generally agreed to them. But Don was obviously disappointed in my lack of interest. We tried to split up the jobs by ability. I corresponded to arrange for a pilot to drop our supplies, and I handled most of the food buying. We were both financially cramped, so we had to skimp wherever we could. Fortunately, we arranged to drive someone else's truck to Alaska, so we had free transportation. I managed to get free candy bars and rope in exchange for possible testimonials. We made our own snowshoes, and Don (who was extremely resourceful in this respect) made a bivouac tent, down vests, special clothing attachments, and some extra-long ice pitons, barbed like harpoons, for the extremely rotten ice we knew to expect.

I much preferred climbing to making ice pitons; hence I went on the club's trip nearly every weekend. But I also thought it important that we get into as good shape as possible before we tried anything so difficult as Deborah. With more practice than Don was getting, my climbing quickly got better than his. I climbed often with Matt, and found that I liked rock climbing with him better than with Don. Matt was impatient and quick, like myself; Don was slow and thorough. On one unfortunate weekend, the three of us climbed together

on the same rope. At one point, Don couldn't climb a
section that Matt and I had both managed. We felt em-
barrassed; at the same time, I got annoyed as Don
made excuses about the heat. But it was obvious that he
was not feeling well. What I ignored was the fact that
Don simply could not get into good shape as long as his
school situation was so distasteful—the East genuinely
oppressed him. What he ignored was the silliness of his
own rationalizations about this problem.

Our rift deepened. We had to meet often to talk
about plans; but whereas in March the hostilities would
develop as we talked, in April and May the hostility
was there to begin with. I found it hard even to talk to
Don. His slow, deliberate way made me terribly impatient; on the other hand, he began to distrust my impatience and felt that he had to be careful and thorough
to cover up for what I should overlook in my haste. At
the same time, I was turning more and more toward
Matt for friendship.

Don and I both knew how badly things were going.
Yet we persisted in planning for Deborah almost with a
kind of fatalism. It was I who tended to provoke the
arguments between us; I knew vaguely that I was using
Don simply as a release for hostilities I felt toward a
hundred different things, but I could not change the
fact. Yet it was obvious the expedition would be unpleasant, maybe even a disaster, if we continued this
way. In a friendlier moment I told Don that I thought
the problems would tend to vanish once we were actually climbing. But he was not so sure. Later he told me

that he had come close to calling it all off; he had talked it over with his roommates, who had suggested that. But perhaps out of the same mixture of loyalty and fatalism that I felt, Don didn't call it off. Instead, he wrote me a long letter. He gave it to me one day and asked me to read it. It was absurd, I thought, that things had come to this, that we could not even talk out our problems. But I read the letter. In it Don said, in part, "As we are committed to each other to climb Mt. Deborah as a team, fruitless arguments must be eliminated . . . I am sure we have sufficient experience in this sort of climbing. I am also confident that we can rise to the occasion. . . . We are undefeatable. . . . It is immensely important that we understand and respect each other and his judgment." As little as I wanted to admit it, I was moved. For one thing, I had not realized that Don understood my feelings, because he tended to disguise his perception of them. For another, I was moved by the tone of the letter: Don's affection for me showed plainly; it made me nostalgic for the easier days of our friendship, when we talked indefinitely about mountains all over the world we would climb together.

Although I did not give Don the answer he probably hoped for, things seemed to improve somewhat after that. Gradually I got more involved in the planning, as the shortness of our time demanded it. Then came Harvard's reading period, in May, at the end of which we would take finals. I got my studying done, but Don almost threw up his hands in despair. He could not do both things at once, and Deborah was more important.

During the last, hectic days, we spent almost all our time in the clubroom. While Don made equipment, I packed all our food into plastic bags and boxes for the airdrop. For compactness and lightness, and to save money, we had planned a minimum of food: less than two pounds per man per day. But we reasoned, on the basis of our Christmas trip, that this would be plenty to keep us going.

During the last week we stayed up most of the nights, working virtually without rest. Matt dropped by often to chat with us. He seemed to be sorry he wasn't going himself, yet I think he was convinced that Don and I were going to get along so poorly that the expedition would be very little fun. We took breaks from the packing only to go to finals and meals. On my birthday I spent a few hours with a girl from Radcliffe. Don said he didn't mind; but he must have thought it a little frivolous. As I walked my date back to her dorm, in the warm sun of a late spring afternoon, we talked about classes and friends and the next year; Deborah seemed impossibly remote. It was then that I realized how I was approaching the expedition: as an arduous adventure to get through with, a thing to be conquered, a place to visit for the sake of wonder and beauty, but from which to return when it began to wear thin. If I had thought carefully, I might then have seen that for Don the expedition was just the opposite: an adventure to be lived as long as possible, a place to go where he could be at home and relax, almost like home itself. If I had understood that, perhaps I could have understood what lay behind many of the intense antagonisms we were to go through on Deborah. But perhaps even then we couldn't have prevented them.

At last, at noon one day in early June, we were ready to go. We had a last ritual beer together, then climbed, exhausted, into our truck, and started driving westward.

3 ▲

A few miles out of Boston we ran out of gas. Fortunately, we had just passed a service station and it didn't take long to get moving again. We were hoping to drive straight through to Alaska, since we had planned to meet our pilot on June 10, less than six days away. At first the driving was pleasant, and we could relax from the frantic pace of packing. Don seemed to cheer up the moment we left New England, and to grow happier and happier the farther west we got. We took turns driving every three hours or so. All our gear was packed in the back of the pickup, which barely held it; to sleep, we had to lie half curled up on the seat. It wasn't very comfortable, but at first we could have slept anywhere.

The turnpikes took us quickly through the night, across New York, Ohio, and Indiana. Then we circled Chicago and headed northward into Wisconsin. It was a fine, sunny day; we felt particularly cheerful and benevolently gave a hitchhiker a short ride. In an area called the Wisconsin Dells, we drove off on dirt side roads to reach one of the strange sandstone towers that dot the flat countryside there. For a delightful hour we climbed various routes on the crumbly rock, roping up for the harder ones. Hardly practice for Deborah, but it was a welcome interlude in the monotonous driving.

It was Sunday. That night, just before midnight, we were driving into the outskirts of Minneapolis. I pulled out to pass a car dragging a boat on a trailer. Two jolly-looking men in the car yelled something at us and I yelled back as I pulled in front of them. They immediately pulled out and passed us back; the man on the right-hand side leaned out the window to shout something. Then they pulled off on the shoulder of the road. I thought they were trying to tell us there was something wrong with our tires or the load, so I pulled off just ahead of them and started to get out. But Don, who had been looking back, said, "Hold it!" I turned to look, and saw the man who had yelled running up toward our truck; as he got near, we could hear him screaming obscenities. Don locked the door an instant before the man grabbed the handle. In the dark I saw a furious, brutish face screaming at us. The man started kicking the side of the truck. I put the truck in gear and shot off, spraying gravel behind. Don, watching, saw the man run back to the car and jump in.

For about ten miles they chased us. Neither of our vehicles could go faster than fifty, so we stayed just ahead of them. But we couldn't lose them. Eventually we had to stop at a red light where cars were lined up in front of us. Moments later, the men appeared behind us. Again the maniac jumped out. We had the doors locked, but couldn't move. I started blowing the horn. The man jerked fiercely on the door, yelling with almost berserk fury, while Don sat there helpless. Then the man began hitting the window with his fist. Just as it shattered, the light changed and I could start off again.

They chased us through the darkened residential streets of Minneapolis. I ran red lights and stop signs, afraid to pause, driving recklessly. We looked desperately for an open store or a gas station. Don kept peering back and reported them always just behind us. At last we saw a lighted gas station. I careened toward it as Don opened the window and yelled, "Call the police! Call the police!"

A stupefied attendant looked up and froze. The men with the boat started to follow us into the station, then swerved and took off down a side street. Breathlessly, we told the attendant what had happened and used his phone to call the police. They sounded slightly skeptical but promised to look for the men. Don and I were still irrationally afraid they would return. After half an hour, we started on. The window was shattered but still held together. The door was slightly dented.

We left Minneapolis and headed into the dark again, wondering what we had done to provoke the men. Perhaps they had just been on the way home, drunk and belligerent after a Sunday outing. Laughing nervously, we told each other that we had better get up to Deborah in a hurry—driving was too dangerous. In the early morning darkness, after the excitement, neither of us could sleep. We began to feel quite happy; the dark was comfortable, and we were glad to be alone, moving away from people, toward mountains and vast stretches of barren tundra and subarctic nights without darkness.

The countryside grew more and more desolate. We loved it: the open, dusty land spoke of the true West to us. The next morning found us crossing North Dakota. We got to the border station in the afternoon. The customs man asked us if we were carrying any alcoholic beverages. "No," I said, just as Don also started to answer. We looked at each other. The customs man eyes us sharply. "Just a half pint of brandy," I admitted; with a sinking feeling I could imagine digging through all our carefully packed boxes to find it. "For medicinal purposes, of course," the man said. "Have a good trip, boys."

So we were in Canada. If anything, Saskatchewan looked bleaker than North Dakota. We drove mile after monotonous mile, beginning to feel tired and listless. But the weather grew splendid again. In the afternoon we approached the Canadian Rockies; for an hour we gazed at the shimmering white peaks in the distance, picking out glaciers and summits among them. We tried to identify the highest ones: that looked like Alberta, and perhaps the other one, on the left, was Edith Cavell. All at once we noticed that one of the glaciers seemed to be moving before our eyes. Sheepishly, we realized that we'd been looking at a bank of clouds, not a mountain range.

From Calgary we headed north to Edmonton, the last big city on our route. There we bought final supplies for the Alaska Highway. Don pointed out how friendly the people were compared with Easterners; my disagreement provoked a short argument.

Soon after leaving Edmonton, we began to feel the toll of continuous driving. It was hard to sleep well on the seat; every bend in the road jostled the sleeper. We developed a kind of paranoia about having to take our turns driving; when we slept, we dreamed about going off the road. Several times Don woke up with a start and lunged for the wheel to save us.

Moreover, as we got more tired, we felt we had to spend all our spare time sleeping, so the driver seldom had the other to talk to. But the nondriver would be afraid the absence of conversation would make the driver sleepy, so he would try to stay awake, chatting, as long as he could. Typically, for instance, if I was driving, Don would lie down, saying, "I'm just going to doze off for a while." I would murmur an O.K. A few minutes later Don would say sleepily, "Feel free to

▲ 41

wake me up if you get sleepy." I would answer, "It's all right, I'm wide awake," even though I was wondering how much longer I could keep my eyes open. "You go ahead and catch some sleep," I would continue, "you'll have to drive soon enough." At last Don would relax and fall asleep. After what always seemed to him only two or three minutes, I would pull over. As Don woke up, I would say, "Your turn." He would ask, suspiciously glancing at the mileage, "How far did you make?" Then he would groggily get behind the wheel while I tried to sleep, and the roles would be reversed.

At midnight, under a spectacular display of aurora, we reached Dawson Creek, where the Alaska Highway begins—twelve hundred miles of dirt road winding through British Columbia and the Yukon. Until now we had been able to average fifty mph, but henceforth we hovered around thirty. The standard two-hundred-mile shift was too long now; we had trouble covering a hundred miles at a stretch. We took NōDōz tablets, but they actually seemed to put us to sleep; perhaps whenever we took them we relaxed, counting on the stimulation.

The next day we stopped at Liard Hot Springs, five hundred miles along the highway, and soaked for an hour in the steamy baths. Don seemed unusually morose. We had been under tension for the last two days. On the way back to the truck, he insisted that we take the driving more slowly and stop to sleep part of each night. There was no point getting to Alaska exhausted, he said, and driving when we were sleepy was dangerous. This was true, but I was secretly glad Don had admitted the strain before I had. I pretended that the driving didn't bother me. I was extremely impatient to get to Alaska; so I argued that we had to meet our pilot on time. We drove on, but the argument waxed bitterly. All our hostilities came out; we accused each other of things that had nothing to do with the driving. Don was truly exhausted and seemed close to tears. In reaction, I grew as cold and heartless as I could; I said that if Don couldn't take the pace, I would drive all the way myself. The argument ended without a compromise, and we sat in silent hostility for hours. This was different from our arguments at Harvard; here we could not get away from each other. It was the first hint of what the bad moments of the expedition itself would be like. We sat in the same small, contained space, just as later, during storms, we would lie in our tent, only a few feet away from each other, with no one else to talk to, wordlessly furious at each other.

But now and then we could relax and enjoy the trip. Though we had not driven together the year before, each of us remembered hundreds of spots along the road. Much of the little conversation we did have dwelt on these memories; we could discuss for fifteen minutes whether or not a given mountain had had more snow on it the year before. We bought a huge piece of cheap steak in Whitehorse and cooked it beside a swamp along the road: for a while it was just like a picnic. I gave in to Don one night and we spread our sleeping bags on the ground for a good five-hour nap.

I was driving just before sunset, on our sixth day out of Boston, as we neared the border of Alaska. The sun was setting straight ahead of us in a prolonged blaze of orange: it was hard to see the road, but the evening was dazzlingly beautiful. Don kept waking up to admire the sight. For the first time we really felt we were in the north country: it was after 10:00 P.M., and the sun was taking hours to set as it obliquely angled toward the horizon. The long drive was almost over, and we could forget some of the disagreements that had made us quarrel.

In the early morning of June 12, we reached Marvin Warbelow's house and airstrip, a few hundred miles into Alaska. We knew him only by correspondence. He was glad to meet us, hadn't worried about time, and wasn't in any rush to do the airdrop. A dark-haired, folksy man of about forty, he loved to talk; he had grown up in Minnesota, but that was too crowded for him—he intended never to leave Alaska. His equally talkative wife claimed that Marvin was so antisocial that he'd only worn a suit once in his life, at his own wedding. Don took to him immediately; I liked him but had reservations because his lack of haste seemed inefficient to me.

In a final burst of activity, we double-boxed all our supplies for the airdrop. Don was to fly with Warbelow as soon as the weather allowed; meanwhile I would drive to Fairbanks to pick up our portable radio. We got the packing done in a few hours. Don and I drove to an airport that evening to meet Warbelow, who was

South-Central Alaska

going to look the weather over. When he got there, he said they would have to wait. He flew Don back to his airstrip with him while I drove to Fairbanks. Before I left, I had pestered Warbelow for a guess when he could fly. In true Alaskan bush-pilot tradition, he was noncommittal. Later he observed to Don, "Your friend's a mighty impatient fellow, isn't he?"

On the drive to Fairbanks, I felt a relief to be alone for a change. I stopped the truck on the bridge over the Tanana River, which was in flood, and got out. I was standing only about fifty miles north of the Hayes Range but Deborah was hidden by thick clouds. The river thundered under the bridge, carrying huge trees with it like little twigs. The river made me imagine Deborah. For a moment I felt a heavy foreboding about the whole thing. Here we were, before the trip had even begun, already glad to get away from each other for a while. Nothing could have seemed further from the easy camaraderie we had felt before McKinley.

But it was a fruitless speculation. I reached Fairbanks the next morning and quickly picked up the radio and last-minute supplies. Now there was nothing to do but wait for Don, who would take the bus to Fairbanks as soon as he had finished the airdrop. On the second bus, I got a note from him: they couldn't fly because the bad weather was still prevailing. There was no telling how long they would have to wait.

A friend I had written to arranged for me to stay in a dormitory at the University of Alaska. I had only my climbing clothes, but I could take a shower and sleep in a clean bed; the change was welcome. As impatient as ever, still I looked forward to the rest. My only duty was to meet the bus every day. And every day Don failed to show up. I spent long hours, especially around midnight, when the light was soft and mysterious, lying on the campus grass, reading. Had it been clear, I could have seen Deborah from there, nearly a hundred miles away; but the mountain was always lost in clouds. During the day I listened to records on a phonograph in the library or browsed through the stores of Fairbanks. I wrote a high-spirited letter to the Radcliffe girl and a letter to Matt, telling him that already Don and I had had serious arguments—I also asked Matt if he would like to plan a trip in the Colorado Rockies, in late August, when I got back.

Nothing could have seemed less like a prelude to an expedition. Don, waiting at Warbelow's, was enjoying the rest immensely. He hiked off one night and made a bold solo ascent of a difficult unclimbed, unnamed peak. For the first time that year he felt he was getting into good shape.

I waited five days. At last, on June 17, Don arrived; Warbelow and he had just done the airdrop that morning. He was unrestrainably excited about the mountains —they were spectacular beyond all our dreams. But Deborah! In a grave voice, Don warned me, "We're in for something incredible, Dave."

We packed up what we would be carrying on the hike-in: all the equipment that we would need to get to base camp, eight days' food, and everything, like the radio, that was too valuable to have risked in the drop. We left Fairbanks and drove all night again to reach the Denali Highway. It was a clear, cool day; at 3:00 A.M. we saw no other cars on the road. We reached Susitna Lodge, the only house for forty miles, around six in the morning. The owner was just getting up. Explaining who we were, we asked him to drive us about ten miles farther down the road, then bring the truck back to his lodge, where it would be picked up later. The man, himself a bush pilot and big-game guide, might have thought we were crazy if he hadn't often felt the same sort of urge we did, hadn't seen Deborah from the air, and hadn't grown to love all the country surrounding it. "Just the two of you, eh?" he said, bemused. We had coffee; then he drove us the ten miles down the road. He parked on the shoulder, helped us lift our seventy-five-pound packs out of the truck, wished us luck, and drove off.

4 ▲

We faced about a forty-mile hike in. For the first fifteen
miles we would cross level tundra, swamp, and gravel
bar to reach the mouth of the West Fork Glacier. Then
we had to ascend the glacier twenty-five miles until at
last we would round a corner of Mount Deborah and
overlook our airdrop site, which would become base
camp. Don said that the Deborah drop had gone off
well; Warbelow had had just enough room to circle
over the glacier while Don pushed the boxes out from
only about sixty feet up. But the second drop, west of
Mount Hayes, hadn't gone so smoothly. The basin was
so narrow that Warbelow couldn't circle within it; in

fact, he doubted that he would have tried the drop at all, given a second chance. At last they had had to throw supplies out from about three thousand feet above the glacier, attached to a parachute. Don had seen the parachute fall but never quite saw it land, and couldn't be exactly sure where it had come to rest. This was a crucial disadvantage, for a month later the supplies might well be buried under new snow.

It was seven-thirty in the morning of June 18, a fine, warm day. We put on our heavy packs, groaning competitively under the loads. Without a glance back, Don started off through the spongy grass on the side of the road; I followed him. The mosquitoes were scarce, and for several miles the muskeg we walked on stayed decently dry. We crossed several shining brooks, taking off our boots to wade them barefoot. Instead of a nuisance, the glacial water was a refreshing shock. We were both, apparently, in good shape and went for hours without a rest. And it took hours for the pleasure of hiking to wear off, hours before our shoulders noticed the loads or our legs the pace. Around noon, the sky clouded up, threatening rain. The ground had gradually been getting wetter, which slowed our pace. We had to look for drier, slightly raised ridges of ground and often had to detour around large swamps. We could no longer hope to keep our feet dry but waded obliviously through the ankle-deep ooze. Our feet made sloppy sucking noises and splattered our pants with mud. It was hard work and we could average only about one mile an hour.

I was getting not only tired, but sleepy, since I had

done most of the driving through the previous night. We stopped for a rest on a dry log, facing a particularly large swamp, through which we could see no easy route. After a few minutes Don got up. "I'll just go ahead a little to look things over," he said. I answered that I'd follow in a minute or two. The sun was out again; I felt too warm and comfortable to move.

I fell asleep. When I woke, I couldn't tell if it was thirty seconds or half an hour later. Don was nowhere in sight. The sleep had disoriented me. I got to my feet, looking around; for a moment I couldn't remember which way we'd been going. Then I recognized the swamp. I put on my pack and started off. For a while I could see a faint track of Don's steps through the water and weeds, but I soon lost it. I stopped and shouted Don's name. There was no answer. It seemed silly, but I felt the edge of panic and I felt terribly lonely. I could imagine Don stopping to wait for me ahead, while I, going a different direction, went past him and on toward the glacier. Don might go back to look for me, might even return all the way to the road, while I wandered around the snout of the glacier, shouting and searching. What an absurd beginning that would be! I hurried on, stopping to shout every now and then. To get around the swamp, I had to go somewhat out of the line we had been following before. For the first time I appreciated how huge the country was and how lost a single person inevitably was in it.

Perhaps twenty minutes later I heard an answer to one of my shouts. With great relief I followed it until,

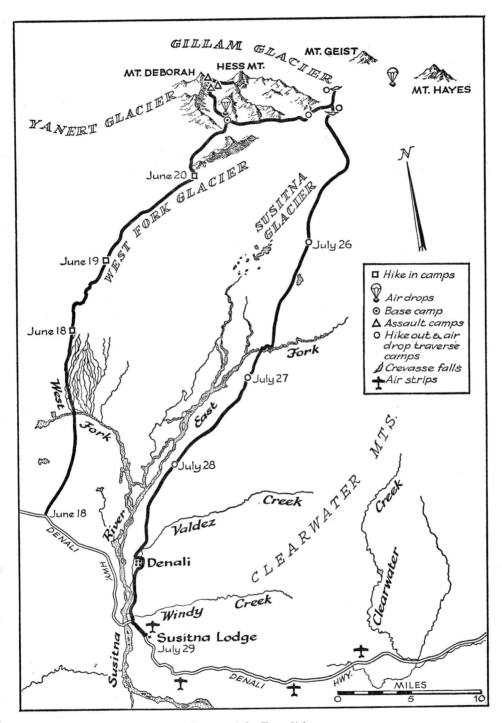

Route of the Expedition

quite far off, I saw Don standing beside a tree. He looked so tiny; the tree could have been any of a thousand; there was no way of singling it out in this landmarkless country. Don waited for me, a bit impatient perhaps. I joined him with a sheepish feeling; but we decided to be more careful from now on about splitting up.

At last the tundra sloped downward to the broad sandbar of the West Fork River. We could see, stretching into the distance, five miles of perfectly flat sand, through which wove the many braids of the river. At 3:00 P.M. we put down our packs before the first of the many little streams and ate a breakfast from our food box. We spread our sleeping pads, then napped for three hours. Afterwards, we started on. The weather was clearing, and the late afternoon sun highlighted the rugged mountains ahead of us. The sand was the easiest going yet; we could make a steady three miles an hour. The nap had refreshed us, and once again moving was a pleasure. A crust of ice lay on some of the river bed, allowing us to cross many of the little streams without even getting our boots wet.

After an hour we spotted some animals, running away from us, about half a mile ahead. Stopping to look carefully, we saw that they were grizzlies. Every so often the largest one would stop abruptly, turn, and rear toweringly on its hind legs to look back at us. Apparently they were a mother and two cubs, the worst possible combination. But they showed no signs of turning on us. Even half a mile away, we could see the awesomely powerful muscles in the mother's back ripple as she ran. We remembered that the bush pilot had told us we should carry a gun in this terrain. As we walked, we kept an eye on the grizzlies until they were too remote to see; meanwhile we talked about methods of defense: Could we stand back to back warding them off with ice axes? Or dodge their rushes, like touch-football players? We felt naked and vulnerable, without a tree for miles around; but perhaps the very openness had made the grizzlies see us from a distance and flee instead of attacking.

We stopped at 10:20 P.M., with the end of the glacier only a mile ahead. We had covered about fifteen miles this first day and felt tired and satisfied. In the placid twilight we gathered sticks and built a comfortable fire. As we had learned from McKinley, nothing could dispel the loneliness of the huge flatlands like a fire, especially at dusk. We cooked in great leisure, drying our boots before the flames. For the first time since Christmas I felt the wonderful, easy companionship that Don and I had discovered then. The first day had gone well, without a harsh word between us. The darkening sky was still clear and we had forgotten about the grizzlies. I recognized the still-strong habits of civilization: the sudden urge for an ice-cream cone or the baseball scores, the reliance on clocks and surrounding noise for mental security, so that the silence and changelessness of this spot where we were camped seemed bleak and alien. But I was happy, too: Deborah, after all the preparation, was becoming a reality.

Instead of the tent, we set up only our plastic rain fly, propping it up like an open tent with our packs. We got into our sleeping bags and quickly fell asleep.

During the night I awoke to the sound of big drops of rain hitting the fly. Somehow, in a matter of hours, a storm had moved in. I fumbled for Don's watch, which we kept between us; since it was still the middle of the night, I crawled farther under the plastic roof and fell asleep again. In the gray light of morning I woke to find it still raining, steadily and hard. I felt depressed. We decided to wait till the rain showed signs of stopping; I welcomed the chance to rest. My shoulders ached from the pack, and I was developing slightly sore hips from the rubbing of the waist loop.

For hours, while Don continued to sleep, I lay awake watching the rain. We could stay completely dry; hence it was fascinating to see the water falling directly above our heads, to watch it splash on the plastic, then trickle toward the ground. There were several little pools of water where the sheet sagged; I would pick a particular drop and try to guess which pool it would end up in. Sometimes there was real suspense as a little bead of water poised above a crucial junction, resisted nudges, and at last hurtled down the plastic slope. I tried to imagine the drop of water with a mind of its own; but there was such random abandon to its motion that I could not. I tried to imagine all the drops that had fallen here, in all the millennia before this day, with no one to watch them, or all the drops that were falling now beyond my vision, on Deborah itself, for instance.

The effort depressed me further; there was such a mind-less vastness to the rain, as to this country, that I, with purposes and memories, felt ineffectual and silly by comparison. I read a book for a while but went back to watching the rain because it seemed more interesting

In the middle of the day Don discovered that he'd left his boots out in the rain, beside the coals of last night's fire. He dashed out to get them, then brought them back under the fly, lamenting that they were soaked through. We ate lunch slowly, waiting for the rain to ease up. At last, around 4:30 P.M., it stopped. It seemed an unusual time to start out but we did so anyway. The sky was gloomy and overcast; in the dim light the rubble-strewn snout of the glacier loomed heavily above us. So much crushed rock had collected there on top of the ice that a few weeds, and one scrawny tree, grew out of it. In a few years the tree would probably plunge, uprooted, off the edge of the glacier; but no one would be there to see such a major event.

We followed the western edge of the glacier for two miles, as the slope of a low mountain gradually pinched us in. For a while we had a good caribou or sheep trail to follow, but it gradually got lost in the rocks. At last we climbed onto the glacier. For about a mile we wound our way through piles of shattered rock, occasionally scraping through to the hard ice underneath. We came to only one obstacle, a swift glacial stream that cut a deep channel down the glacier. There was no question of wading it, because the bottom would be polished ice.

We wandered up and down the edge for a while until Don found a bed where the stream undercut the near bank. He took off his pack and jumped easily down and across. I handed him the packs, then jumped myself. Of course we were not "stuck" on the glacier now, but the irreversibility of our jump pleased us. We knew we would be on glaciers for a long time, that we would have no more wood fires, and, soon, no more running water. But these deprivations were steps in our initiation, steps toward Deborah.

Soon we reached the bare tongue of ice marked on the map. The night was getting darker, but we could easily see where we were going. It was pleasant walking, very slightly uphill. The hard ice had a rough surface, like asphalt. To relieve the monotony, it was pocked everywhere with thimble-sized holes filled with crystal-clear water. Little channels of running water threaded their ways toward the end of the glacier, and here and there a small crevasse lay open.

After about seven hours, we decided to camp. For the first time, we pitched our tent, the small orange tent that Don had designed and made himself. Cooking dinner inside reminded us at once of Christmas, and of McKinley; it was much cozier than lying in the open. We were camped at the only big bend in the glacier. We had made good progress and hoped to reach base camp in another day or two. Again we had got along well, without even the threat of an argument. We slept soundly.

Early the next afternoon we were off again. The

weather was clearing gradually, and for a while we made fast progress. But soon we came to the nevé line, above which the snow had not yet melted down to bare ice. It was wet stuff; we got soaked to our knees in hidden pools of slush. We trudged over to a moraine, where we could follow the long ridge of rock debris that the glacier was imperceptibly carrying downhill. This kept us dry, except where here and there we had to wade a gap of slush; but it was much slower going. We stopped for lunch after a few hours, then continued on our homemade snowshoes, deserting the moraine. As we got higher, the snow turned drier and deeper. Soon we decided to rope up, since the snow might be hiding crevasses. After that we traveled a hundred and fifty feet apart, keeping the rope taut between us.

All the clouds had vanished, and the sun, reflected by snow on all sides, made the glacier actually seem hot. We sweated and put on sunburn cream. The going was extremely monotonous; on both sides we were enclosed by steep, intricate peaks. Although they seemed only a few hundred yards away, we could see from the map that the glacier itself was two miles wide. In demonstration of this trick of scale, we seemed to be walking on a treadmill, so that it took forever for the walls to recede beside us. Ahead we could look at a wall of rock where the glacier split into two forks. There we would take a short cut, the left-hand fork which led past the southeast ridge of Deborah to an easy gap overlooking the airdrop basin. But only after seven hours did we reach the junction. Meanwhile the south face of Deborah had come into view, a sheer five-thousand-foot wall of ominous blue-black rock. Even from six miles away, the wall jutted high into the sky. Don had warned me about the sight, but I was still overwhelmed by my first glimpse of Deborah.

By the time we had reached the junction the sun had set, the glacier had cooled off, and the pale twilight again decorated the mountains with gloomy shadows. We were tired and decided to camp. It would take another day to reach the airdrop. In seven hours of steady hiking we had covered only nine miles.

A breeze sprang up, chilling us as it dried the sweat on our bodies. We pitched the tent quickly and put the rain fly over it, in case it should storm during the night. We were camped near a slushy pool; for the last time we were able to collect water for cooking. After that night, for weeks, we would be melting snow for all our water.

I went to bed feeling depressed and a little bit lonely. The encompassing solitude, the lack of things to say, the contrast of emptiness around us—we had not really felt these on McKinley. The day's work had been dull and arduous. But dinner itself was, as always, a pleasure, and I managed to sleep well afterward.

We got a good start the next morning. The going was the same, slow and monotonous, but the slope gradually steepened as we neared the southeast gap. Soon we came upon the tracks of some animal, apparently a bear. Don had seen them from the air, apparently fresh, six days before; now they were faded, having melted and broadened into the snow. They led, very purposefully, up to our gap; we followed them. It seemed incredible that a bear should have been so far up on the glacier; what could he have eaten, and where was he headed? On the other hand, what sense would a bear have made of our footprints?

After three hours we reached the gap. Stepping through it, we came at once into sight of the immense and frightening east wall of Deborah, at the far end of which we could see the precipitous line of plastered ice that marked our route, the east ridge. As I wrote in my diary that night, "Descriptions fail. It is going to be tough." We could also see, only a mile away, our airdrop, a scattering of boxes on the flat snow.

Our first argument had been brewing. The pretext was a trifle: I got annoyed because Don had used the phrase "well-behaved" four or five times to describe the glacier's lack of crevasses. Absurdly, then, as we walked the last mile to base camp, under the stupendous shadow of Deborah, we irritably argued the merits of the word "well-behaved." What had really provoked the quarrel, I suppose, was the boredom of the hiking. I had started to notice some of Don's mannerisms and, for lack of a better preoccupation, had picked on one of them to vent my frustrations. It was the first time that I recognized a trait of my own, which seemed to me in analysis almost diabolical. I could not stand for things to go well for too long a stretch; it was as if I needed a regular exercise of hostility. Don realized this need in me but could not understand it. Later it would intensify and work itself out in unexpected guises.

But reaching the boxes diverted our attention. We gathered them up, pleased to find almost no damage from impact and nothing lost. In the afternoon we pitched our tent there, at 6300 feet, two miles south of the east ridge of Deborah. Beside the tent were stacked ten boxes, each containing food for the two of us for four days. We were alone and self-sufficient; we could not use the radio until we reached the ridge at 9400 feet, for it required a direct line to Fairbanks. All our climbing equipment, including three thousand feet of fixed rope, eighty pitons, and hammers and carabiners and slings and stirrups, was piled there with us. We also had a few paperback books, the newspapers we had stuffed the airdrop boxes with, full of two-week-old news, our diaries and a few pencils, and, in with the food, a half pint of "victory brandy"—actually, an apricot liqueur we had bought on the last day in Cambridge.

We planned to shift to a nighttime schedule, to take advantage of slightly colder temperatures and crisper, safer snow. That night we would start hauling supplies to the top of the basin, directly under the dark mountain wall. I got into the tent to read. Don had found that the long aluminum pole we had dropped in to mark base camp made a natural trumpet. For an hour he blurted wild peals toward Deborah, which echoed them magnificently. The basin, which for aeons had overheard only the clatter of an occasional falling rock, or the rumble of an avalanche, or the whine of wind or the murmur of falling snow, became for a brief hour an auditorium for stranger cries than any animal had ever made. Don loved it; he was home at last.

5 ▲

That night, the first of summer, we set out with hopes
not only of relaying loads but of starting the climbing
itself. As we had found before, however, the distances
were deceiving. It took us two hours just to get to the
head of our basin. The snow was crisp and dry, but we
had to find a path through a series of large crevasses
that blocked the way. In the dull light of night the glacier looked featureless until we were almost upon the
crevasses. It was no trouble to avoid the open ones;
what scared us was the possibility of a thinly covered,
hidden one through which we might suddenly plunge.

However, we had no trouble that night. At an altitude of 7500 feet, just under the towering wall, we dumped our little cache of supplies.

Two thousand feet above us was a shelf of snow, or col, where the east ridge dipped lowest between Deborah and nearby Mount Hess. It was on the col that we planned to place our advance camp, from which the final assault could proceed. But it was clear to us that simply getting to the col would be quite a problem. To go straight up would have been to climb a steep wall of snow and rock, often swept by avalanches. Even if we could climb this headwall, it would be hellish to carry supplies up it. The alternative was to climb the shoulder of Mount Hess, actually reaching a point a full thousand feet above the intended col, then to descend toward Deborah along the ridge until we reached the col. But this, too, was a tricky proposition. That night we decided only to haul another load up to the point we had reached, which would become Camp I.

The trip back was quick, but we found the second trip grueling. We set a fast pace because we wanted to keep warm. But when we reached the cache spot again, a stiff wind met us. We would have liked to rest, but as soon as we sat down we started shivering; hence we turned back right away toward base camp. Both loads had taken us a full six hours, which was rather discouraging progress. But base camp cheered us up. Soon the sun rose and it grew comfortably warm. We moved our rubber pads outside the tent, where we could sun-bathe on them while we cooked dinner. The incongruities of a

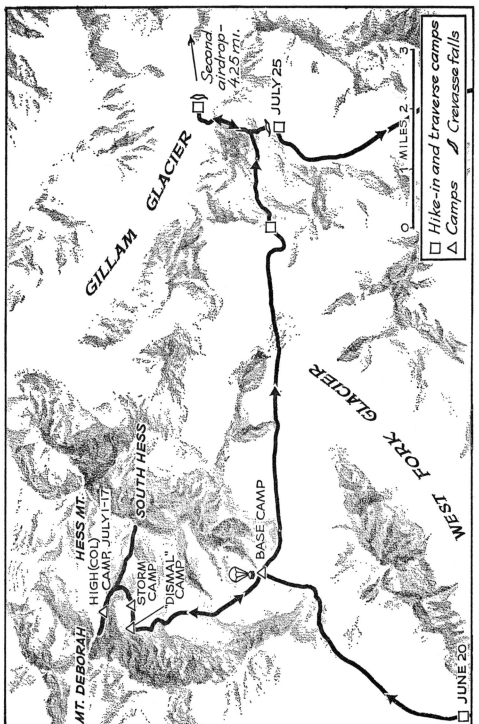

Route of the Attempt

night-climbing schedule were familiar to us from Mc-
Kinley; so was the hot glacial sun, which could grow
even stiflingly hot during the day. Thus this pleasant
basking seemed to us one of the privileges we earned by
working at night. Had we been told that this was to be
the last truly warm day we would have on the whole
expedition, we would not have believed it. So far, after
all, the weather had been good; except for the day of
rain, we had had basically clear skies. It was much the
same sort of weather we had enjoyed on McKinley.

That evening, the sky began to cloud up. We had
managed, before the sun set behind the huge east wall
of Deborah, around 2:00 P.M., to dry our boots for
the first time in four days. But by 9:00 P.M., when we
were ready to set out, a mist had descended; a warm
wind blew rainy snow across the basin, and our boots
got wet immediately when we began hiking. We managed, with very heavy loads, to carry everything else we
would need for the route; thus we could abandon base
camp in favor of Camp I. We left eight days' food and
some gasoline at base camp: provisions for the traverse
to our second airdrop, later, with a slight margin for
safety.

We moved very slowly up the basin, uneasy because
of the mushy snow surface. It was obviously too miserable to explore higher, so we pitched the tent at our
cache and got inside. The site had an immediately de-
pressing effect on me. I felt at the bottom of a chasm
formed by the surrounding walls. We would only get a
few hours' sunlight on a clear day, and we had a

cramped view of things. But despite all the shelter of the huge walls around it, the place was almost continuously swept by winds. We had spent only a few hours there that night when I wrote in my diary, "It is a gloomy spot, a place we would call dismal if we had to spend too much time in it."

Instead of letting up, the storm increased. For eighteen hours high winds shook the tent. We dozed fitfully, to the sound of wind rippling the nylon walls. For a while it was relaxing to have only to eat, sleep, and read. Even at midnight it was light enough to read inside the tent. We had counted on this; only in the second airdrop had we bothered with flashlights or candles. Of course, we had to go outside occasionally to relieve ourselves; in the strong winds it was a bitter task. On the night of the 23rd, just as the winds seemed to be letting up, snow began falling. It continued monotonously for another eighteen hours. We could watch the snow level rise slowly along the side of the tent. During the afternoon of June 24, the winds returned. This was a genuine Alaskan storm, taking days to blow itself out. I settled down to read some Fielding and some Hemingway. Passages in the books, especially eating episodes, made me nostalgic for civilization. I reflected that this was only the eighth day of the expedition; it was a bad sign, to be nostalgic already. But I couldn't help it. Don and I were getting along all right, in a negative way. We had little to talk about: we tried one literary conversation, without much heart in it. Don, I knew, was thinking about the mountain, plotting a way to move supplies efficiently and to get us into the best possible position when the storm ended. We might have talked about this; but I was responding to the gloom of the place by ignoring it and didn't want to think about Deborah until we had started climbing on it.

By evening the winds were roaring at high speed again. Don was getting tired of lying down, so he dressed and went out to shovel the snow away from the tent. It took him two hours to do a thorough job because of the winds: occasional gusts nearly knocked him over. When he came back in, his beard and eyelashes were frosted with snow and he dragged snow into the tent with him. He had noticed that a waterfall we had seen earlier, spilling down the east wall, had frozen up.

We slept some more. Gradually the wind died, but the snow continued to fall. About a foot of it had accumulated since we had got there. At last, around noon on the 25th, it started to clear. We were anxious to get out of the tent and start climbing; I, especially, got impatient with the unchanging routine of storm days.

By afternoon it was completely clear. The wall was breathtakingly laced with new snow. We photographed everything in sight, waiting impatiently for night, when the climbing would be safest. The air rang with the thunder of avalanches on the huge east wall, as the new snow was swept off. After the long storm, it looked as if a spell of good weather would be ours. But by the evening the mist had returned and a light snow was falling again. Our spirits took a big drop.

However, it was colder than usual (25°), so we

decided to climb anyway. Eagerly we got dressed and stuffed twenty-five pounds of climbing gear into each of our packs. Instead of snowshoes we put on crampons, since the snow had frozen enough to give their long spikes good purchase. Don started up a steep snow slope toward Mount Hess. I felt as impatient as ever, but excited in a new way. For the first time we weren't carrying back-breaking loads, and for the first time we would really be climbing. With luck, we would reach the col that night. We hadn't lost a serious amount of time during the storm; we were still on schedule.

The snow soon became mixed with rock. I took the lead from Don, who was tired after a long spell of kicking steps. The going was easy; only here and there did we even have to use our hands. But to our dismay, as we touched the rock for the first time, we found it loose and shattered: a blue-gray schist, much like the rotten rock we had encountered on McKinley. In a short while we were out of the rock section. On smooth, steep snow above, we first grew aware of the drop beneath us. The slope was disconcerting, for it was certainly steep enough to avalanche; indeed, on either side of us it had already avalanched. Besides, the texture of it was bad: loose, granular snow often shallowly overlay smooth ice.

As we ascended, the mist had been getting thinner, as if we were near the top of a cloud. We had the feeling we were about to break into clear sky. Don took the lead. He went slowly, chopping steps methodically. After only a few hundred steps he paused, apparently tired. I took the lead again and scrambled over some steep rocks that led to the base of our main obstacle, a large, vertical ice cliff. So far we had not been belaying each other but climbing simultaneously, a rope-length apart. But as Don came up to me, I noticed that he slipped and caught himself. Alarmed (for the slope was easy, if steep), I put him on belay. He came up very slowly, slipping a few more times. When he got to me, I said, "Is there anything the matter? How do you feel?"

"Out of it," he said. "Sleepy . . . and cold."

"How about your balance?"

"That's not too good either." He was looking away from my face. "I don't know what the problem is."

I wanted to go on but I said, "Probably we'd better go down."

Don seemed to agree. I began to build a platform of rocks on which to leave our loads. Suddenly Don said fiercely, "We can't go down, Dave! We've got to make the col. We're losing too much time. I've got to drive myself."

The words startled me. They were so unlike Don, so irrational. Gradually I talked him out of going on, telling him not to feel guilty. He started shivering from the cold. We left our loads on the little shelf I had constructed, tied to a piton I had been able to hammer into the crumbly rock. We were still in mist, but we could see the outlines of the col, at about the same height as we were, toward the northwest. I had brought the radio up. It was possible we were now, just barely, in a direct line with Fairbanks. Before we started down, I tried it. All we heard was static. But we weren't disappointed. Rather than trust the expensive radio to the cache, I carried it with me on the descent.

All the way down, I belayed Don from above. Even on easy places he seemed to be going terribly slowly. At last I lost my patience and asked him to hurry up. He said to me, annoyed, that he felt as if he were racing down the slope. I was disturbed that his sense of time had been so upset. I was sure he was taking four or five times as long as I was, and I attributed it to whatever was making him feel bad. It was only days later, when Don insisted he had been going as fast as I that day, that we realized how differently we had viewed the descent. Don was genuinely astonished that I could have thought he was going four times as slowly as I. When the incident came up, later, in the middle of an argument, each of us was sure he was right. Only gradually did such discrepancies make us start to wonder—what had really happened? How long had it really taken Don? How sick had he acted? Had I exaggerated it, or he underplayed it, or both? On a larger expedition, the truth could never seem so subjective. For the two of us, this uncertainty would subtly add to the fantastic otherworldliness of Deborah. Gradually it would become another danger to guard against. Gradually we would lose a certain sense of our own identities and begin to think more exclusively in terms of reaction to each other.

But as we got lower, Don improved and seemed to

speed up. By the time we had reached camp again he felt fine, though still sleepy. He slept solidly for more than ten hours when we got back.

It was a disappointing beginning. We were still not even near the col. The ice cliff above our highest point didn't look too hard, but it could take a long time. I wondered that I didn't feel more annoyed at Don for halting our progress. But if he was sick, it was nothing to trifle with. And I had almost enjoyed, perhaps in a condescending way, being solicitous toward him, though I knew he would feel in debt to me, in the wrong, resentful way, for it. Perhaps I had been tired myself and was glad of the chance to turn around without having to take the blame for it. I had noticed feeling tired recently—maybe it was the immobility of the storms, or had something to do with our food. But my appetite was fine; in fact, I was ravenously hungry now.

Drearily, it was snowing again. We were bound to spend at least a few more days in this dismal camp. Caches like the one we had made above were unstable; so, for that matter, was the whole dangerous slope we had ascended. There was so much of the climbing left to do. But when we got up high, where mountain climbers belonged, we would do better. Anyway the storms could not last forever: it was bound to clear.

6 ▲

That night, June 26, we woke around eight-thirty.
Within an hour we had cooked breakfast and were
ready to go. But as we walked around outside the tent,
gathering supplies to pack, Don began to feel the same
symptoms that had made him shaky the night before.
We talked over whether or not we should go. We
couldn't decide; Don didn't want to hold us up and I
was impatient to be climbing, but neither of us wanted
to waste a night's effort. At last I suggested a test: we
would run about fifty yards through the deep snow at
top speed and see how Don felt after it. Wallowing

absurdly, we made our little dash. Don didn't feel very good after it, but neither did I. We hemmed and hawed some more and at last decided to go back to bed.

It seemed just as well, for it began to snow again and a moderately brisk wind swept the glacier. We admitted to ourselves that the weather had been worse than usual; but we felt guilty for not seizing the few opportunities we had had. The depression of the dark camp began to infect both of us. We determined to make a strong push the next day. Since the temperature seemed to vary little between day and night, we decided to start in the afternoon instead of in the evening.

With this resolve, we set out at 1:30 P.M., carrying fifty-five to sixty-pound loads. At first we thought we had made a mistake, for the snow was wet and sloppy. As we were climbing the first of the rock, we heard a rumble and saw a small avalanche headed toward us. Leading, I yelled to Don and jabbed the point of my axe into the slope, then crouched, hanging onto it. Some of the slide hit me but I held on; it missed Don below. I felt a tug, which must have come from the weight of the snow catching the rope. I looked down and saw that Don had held his ground. We shouted to each other to confirm that we were all right. Then we continued, nervous about the slopes above. Gradually, though, the snow got colder and safer as the sun left the mountain. Don was feeling strong and we made excellent time.

When we reached the highest point of our previous effort, we found the cache intact. We left our heavy packs attached to the piton, then carried ice-climbing equipment up a little higher to attack the cliff. Almost at once, we realized we had underestimated its severity. The ice was rock hard, and the slope subtly steepened until it was actually vertical. Don chopped the steps on the first pitch. When he reached the end of the rope, he drove a metal screw into the ice for an anchor and brought me up. I made a route-finding mistake by continuing straight up. I had hoped to cross a short steep section head on, but when I got there it bulged out at me, actually overhanging. It would have been far too risky to try it while Don was attached to the mountain only by a flimsy screw and two thousand feet of unbroken slope yawned below us. But for a while I chopped at the ice furiously, swearing out loud as I got more frustrated. Don shouted, "Take it easy, Dave, this is no place to get mad." Sheepishly, I realized what a foolish spectacle it was, cursing a cliff of ice simply for being there, with no one within fifty miles of us in any direction. *That was the old Don!* I thought with gratitude: the sane, careful, competent Don. I put in an ice screw and belayed Don while he chopped a diagonal traverse to the left. It was awkward and difficult, but he did it adroitly. Still, it took a long time for the whole pitch, and I grew uncomfortably cold, standing on my little niche of ice. The mist had lowered just beneath us and the sun was setting beyond Deborah in the northwest: a soft, rosy light spangled the ice all around us. Facing out, I could occasionally let go of the rope with one hand to take pictures. Don rounded a corner, out of sight. For a long time I could only hear him chopping and watch the little chips of ice dance dizzyingly down the slope into the darkness. At last Don shouted, "On belay!" and I could follow. Only by chopping vigorously as I led the next pitch did I get warm. Don's stance was right below me; the chips I knocked loose bounced down on him. The sun had set by now, and he soon got even colder than I had. I could actually see him shivering, and his voice shook with the cold when he talked. But I was on a 60° slope and had to fashion each step carefully. At the top of my pitch, I found that an ice screw would not hold. Instead, I hammered in the first of Don's special aluminum daggers. It was a godsend, the solidest anchor we had yet found on the mountain. We were only about forty feet below the top of the cliff, but the last stretch was the steepest of all. Don led it very nicely. At the top he had to pause on his ice steps while he reached high with his axe to scrape away a lip of rotten snow. At last he was up. I followed him and dashed up another short pitch on steep snow. We were approaching exhaustion, having gone for twelve hours straight without food or a drop of water.

We turned back to descend. On the way down we attached light manila ropes to the screws and dagger, as handlines for the next time we should have to climb the cliff. When we got to the bottom of the ice, where we had left out packs, we could relax somewhat and eat our lunches. We emptied our packs, stashing our supplies in the cache, which was reaching formidable size. Again I had brought the radio. On a hunch I decided to try it again. Turning it on, we were amazed to hear at once clear voices chatting casually. I tried to broadcast; the receiving person heard something but could not make out my words. We soon realized that we were speaking to someone not in Fairbanks, but in Anchorage, almost two hundred miles to the south. Because of the distance, we could not broadcast clearly, it seemed. I tried to get across the words "O.K." and "Portable Seven" (our number), but at last I gave up and signed off with a doubtlessly unintelligible "thank you." The one-sided conversation excited us but also somehow disappointed us; perhaps overhearing someone talk about banal, urban matters while we were perched on an unexplored mountain in the dark of early morning was too much of a contrast.

The candy bars and lemon drops we had for lunch seemed a precious gift; but we got cold quickly and had to start descending before we felt rested. All the way down, the snow was beautifully firm, making the going as easy as we could have wished. Perhaps the cold was a sign of improving weather, we thought. We staggered back to our tent at 6:00 A.M., after sixteen and a half hours of hard climbing, certainly our most demanding day yet on the expedition. We had climbed some difficult pitches of ice; but we were still a long way from the col. That night we hoped to leave our "dismal" camp for good, carrying the tent up and over the ice cliff, pushing for the col, even if it meant another long day. As it always seemed when there was a lot of work to do, we were getting along well. We were too tired to have disagreements. When we got back to camp, it was all we could do to cook dinner and slide into our bags for a blissful sleep.

It was snowing when we awoke. Looking out of the tent, we could see only a very short distance. We stayed put, discouraged, although after our long push we needed a rest. We read and dozed through the night, constantly checking the weather. The steady snow continued to fall. Sometime the next day, I went outside to relieve myself. I happened to notice the tracks of some small animal passing camp. The line of tiny steps went straight by our food cache, without deviating, within three feet of the corner of the tent, and on toward the headwall of Deborah and, perhaps, some instinctive rendezvous. I had thought that we were the only animals that could live in such an inhospitable place; but here had passed some docile creature, making less sound than we could hear, with no curiosity about us or desire for our food. On the other hand, perhaps the animal was trapped and weak, wandering blindly in these cold recesses in a last attempt to find its way off the glacier. We never saw the animal itself.

At 10:00 P.M. on the 29th, we resolved to leave camp. In the confusing mist, we packed up our tent and the last of the supplies that we would need above. We left our snowshoes there; we were worried that we would lose them under the snows that might fall before we got back, but they would have only been an extra burden above. As we left camp, I glanced back. All that marked where we had lived were the crossed snowshoes, stuck upright, and soggy copies of *Joseph An-*

drews and *The Snows of Kiliminjaro* lying there, strangely out of place, on the snow.

We could follow our tracks, but the condition of the snow was very bad. In addition, the blindfold of the mist disconcerted us. It soon became evident that it would be dangerous to climb above; we could hear small avalanches hissing invisibly all around us. But we hated the prospect of returning to camp in the gloomy basin, of wasting our previous efforts.

At last we pitched the tent on a 30° slope beneath the beginning of the rock, between two open crevasses. It was a hazardous site, and we were determined to spend as little time there as possible. We had only a day's food left with us and some odds and ends we could stretch for another day, having carried all the rest up to the cache. We faced the unhappy prospect of having to climb up to the cache simply to bring food back down, food it had taken a considerable effort to carry so high. Moreover, we knew that the steps in the ice cliff, which had cost us so many hours to cut, might well have melted smooth into the cliff, so that we would have to do the chopping all over again.

Thus we camped very discouraged that night, and nervous as well. Sometime the next day we suddenly heard the unmistakable sound of a nearby avalanche. Holding our breaths, we listened as it got louder. We were powerless; we didn't even get out of our sleeping bags. The sound increased, then stopped. Looking out of the tent, we saw that the avalanche had passed by about thirty yards above us. The camp site was no good; but, as the avalanche proved, neither was climbing, so long as the snow continued to fall. And it showed no signs of stopping.

We spent the next night, the last of June, in the same spot. We had eaten the last day's food and were down to the odds and ends. We made a delicious concoction with extra-thick tomato soup and concentrated bacon, but after we had eaten it we were still hungry. Reading had paled. I drew a chessboard in the back of my diary, made little chessmen out of paper, and we played a game. But I played enough better than Don so that the game wasn't much fun.

We would have to climb that night, if only to retrieve food. Deborah itself seemed to be floating away from us; so many unforeseen obstacles had been thrust up in front of us, and the snow, mindlessly monotonous, fell and fell.

In the same kind of weather we packed up and started off at 9:30 P.M. on July 1. But the snow was in good shape, and we traveled fast. It took only two hours to reach the cache. I was leading; just as I got to our supplies, the rope dragging behind me dislodged a rock. I heard it roll down the slope, so I yelled to Don, "Rock!" But it wasn't enough warning. Don ducked, but the rock hit him sharply in the left elbow. He gave a cry of pain and knelt, cradling his arm. Fortunately, the rock had only bruised him, but it was a very painful bruise and hampered him for the rest of the night. I offered to lead all the pitches of the ice cliff, to make it easier for Don.

▲ 77

We picked up a few things from the cache, most importantly the radio and a food box, good for four days. Even the sight of the box reawakened our hunger.

Just at that moment we reached the top of the clouds and broke free of the storm. Like a shipwreck in shallow water, Deborah gleamed in the midnight sun. Even Don, despite the bruise, felt rejuvenated. We had another pleasant surprise: the steps in the ice cliff had filled with loose snow but had retained their shape; it would take no rechopping to use them. The ropes we had left made the going easy, even with our substantial loads. Above the ice we found deep snow, much deeper than the first time we had been there four days earlier. I led the first new pitch, stamping steps quickly in the steep snow. It seemed almost easy enough to justify both of us climbing at the same time; but, after a discussion, we decided it would be wise to continue to belay. We were still on a 45° slope, with the nearly vertical ice cliff now below us.

Don was feeling better, so he started ahead on the next pitch. About forty feet above me, without warning, a hole in the snow appeared under his feet, and he disappeared. I gave him a quick belay, but snow inside the crevasse apparently stopped him first. He yelled that he was O.K.—he had only fallen about fifteen feet. But we were both startled; we wouldn't have believed, until now, that crevasses could exist in the middle of a steep slope—was no part of the mountain safe from them? I tied my end of the rope to my axe and took our spare axe and an extra rope up near the edge of the

1. Deborah, Hess, and South Hess from the south. Base camp, marked with a circle, was approached from the left (solid line) and abandoned, a month later, toward the right. Triangle indicates the high (col) camp just below the east ridge.

2. Deborah and South Hess from the north. Triangle indicates high (col) camp. Approach to the col from the south (dotted line) is out of sight. Mt. Hess itself appears directly in front of South Hess, seemingly all one mountain.

MT. DEBORAH

EAST RIDGE

NORTH FACE

△

▲ High (col) camp

G I L L A M   G L A C I E R

3. The 6000-foot north face of Deborah. East ridge on the left. Triangle indicates col camp, and end of solid line indicates highest point reached.

4. Part of the traverse to the second airdrop, and the beginning of the hike out. The first crevasse is on the Gillam Glacier; the second, only a few miles away, is on the Susitna Glacier, which Roberts and Jensen followed down to the camp of July 26.

MT. HAYES

1st crevasse July 24   2nd airdrop site

July 21-23

2nd crevasse July 25

S U S I T N A   GLACIER

July 26

5. Don Jensen on the third day of the hike-in on the West Fork Glacier. Deborah is not yet in sight.

6. Jensen chopping an ice traverse on the ice cliffs between the Dismal Camp and the col camp. Sun has just risen (1.30 A.M.) in the north.

7. The camp on the col, looking north, before the storms hit.

8. Jensen at the top of the second pitch (rotten rock) on the east ridge.

9. On the east ridge. Looking back, one can see the col camp and climbers' tracks leading across the knife-edged ridge toward the first cliffs (Jensen seconding).

10. Jensen leading a steep traverse in the hollow snow of the east ridge.

11. Jensen seconding on the east ridge below a detached cornice. In the background, crevasses on the Gillam Glacier.

12. Jensen seconding on the most dangerous part of the climb.

13. Jensen eating lunch before the backdrop of the east ridge, on the ascent of South Hess.

14. Looking sideways (south) from the east ridge across the 5000-foot-high east face.

15. Roberts wading the East Fork of the Susitna, at the point at which the climbers finally found a crossing.

crevasse. I threw the rope in. Don tied his pack to it, but I couldn't haul it out. So I retrieved the rope, tied loops in it for footholds and handholds, and lowered it again to Don. He managed to climb up the loops until he was almost out, then helped me pull out his pack. Within an hour we were ready to go again.

When we continued, we were nervous: besides the crevasses, we had avalanches to worry about, and we had to keep our eyes out for the best route. Here and there we could see darker shadings in the snow, where the empty space of a crevasse apparently lurked under a snow bridge like the one Don had broken through. In addition, we noticed when we looked back that it was impossible, except by our tracks, to see where we had come from. If even a light snowfall covered our tracks, then it might be impossible to find the top of the ice cliff, to which the highest fixed rope was attached. How we wished we had brought some of the usual light bamboo stakes to mark the route. But we had a few long aluminum pickets, which we hoped eventually to use for anchors on Deborah; for lack of anything better, we stuck them in the snow every two hundred feet or so, to mark where we had gone.

In the early morning, about 5:00 A.M., we reached the ridge itself, at 10,200 feet. Immediately, we stepped into the warm sunshine. At last we felt we were near Deborah. Besides, the ridge down to the col looked easy. After a comfortable lunch, during which we exchanged enthusiastic predictions, we started down toward it. Just as we were almost there, we suddenly came to a large drop-off, a vertical ice cliff. We couldn't possibly have seen it from above. It was much too high to jump down, and we had no good anchors left to set up a rappel, by which we might have left a rope to slide down and climb back up. Moreover, the cliff stretched, unbroken, across the whole ridge. Finally we had wearily to retrace all our steps back to the point where we had first reached the ridge, detour some forty feet to the north, off the opposite side of the ridge, and hike down a parallel path. As soon as we left the crest of the ridge, we found very deep powder. Our snowshoes would have come in handy here. Instead, we wallowed downward in the hot sunshine, up to our thighs in snow.

But this time we had found an easy route. At 7:00 A.M. we reached the col, a flat shelf of snow that narrowed toward our route. Plastered with new snow, the east ridge of Deborah looked incredibly difficult, but inviting. We set up the tent and made a little cache of supplies beside it. At last we had escaped the pallor of our low, gloomy camps. Before we could start on the route, however, we would have to hike back to the cache at least twice to pick up all our supplies. We were now quite a bit behind schedule but we had twenty days' food to try to get up our route. The weather looked as if it might hold good for a while. Perhaps, as we had found on McKinley, the higher we got, the better the weather would get.

As soon as camp was set up, I tried the radio. It worked perfectly. In clear tones we could hear the people in Fairbanks; they indicated that we came through clearly too. The radio receiver was connectible to the telephone system, so we could call anyone we wanted. We tried a few friends in Fairbanks; then Don decided to call his parents in California. We couldn't quite believe it, and his parents certainly couldn't, but the call went through, and soon Don was chatting with them as casually as if he had called from a corner phone booth in the same town.

We were in tremendous spirits. The radio gave us both a boost; it was as if someone else had dropped by to break up the monotony of our companionship. We felt safer, too, though it was a largely irrational sense of security. The weather was perfect; for the first time, we would be able to watch the sun set and rise from the door of our camp. On the first day we noticed that the sun actually set and rose three times each day: first, it would rise from the horizon in the north, about 1:30 A.M.; then it would set behind the ridge of Mount Hess, which we had just descended, at about eight, re-appearing two hours later. Around two in the after-noon, it would set behind the high crest of Deborah, ris-ing just before five; after that we would get golden sunshine from the northwest until the true sunset, around 11:00 P.M. What place could have been more exciting to live in?

We broke open the food box and cooked a breakfast. With huge appetites we gulped down the food. The work and our enthusiasm, no doubt, were making us hungrier than usual. But there was no danger of our getting fat: if anything, I thought Don looked leaner than before. We were in good shape, as the recent sixteen-and-a-half-hour effort had proved. We couldn't wait to turn loose our energies on Deborah.

7 ▲

Within a matter of hours the sky began to cloud up
again. We lost the edge of exhilaration and optimism
we had begun to feel. By early afternoon the mist had
closed in and it had begun to snow. It snowed for forty
hours straight. We wondered whether it was impossible
to get more than eight consecutive hours' sunshine
here; we had had no more than that for the last ten
days. We lay lethargically in the tent, constantly aware,
with every meal we ate, that our chances of success
were shrinking. We would have been willing to stay
until we could climb Deborah or know that we couldn't,

but our food supply put an absolute limit on our time.

We had reached the col the morning of July 2. That evening, we decided, we would go despite the weather. But at 9:00 P.M., when we got up to leave, the storm was raging. It was 20°—cold enough to numb us, but warm enough so that we felt the painful sting of wetness in the wind, which ripped furiously across the col. There was almost no visibility; particles of ice flayed our faces when we tried to look into the wind. As we stood there, getting bitterly cold, attempting to pack up and put on crampons, it became obvious that we couldn't accomplish anything that night. Shouting to each other over the wind, we called off the effort. I went back inside the tent; Don, eager for exercise, built a snow wall around the tent. The job took hours; he kept yelling to me to inform me of his progress.

After Don came in, we went to sleep for a little while. The snow wall seemed to divert the wind somewhat. But the storm blew just as hard all day on the 3rd. The storm days fouled up our schedule, because we got too much sleep. During them there was nothing by which to mark time except Don's watch. We played a few more chess games and read a while. Little things began to get on my nerves; I got angry at Don because he sometimes lost interest in our chess games. At first I hid my annoyance, simply saying, "Your move," to remind him when he forgot. Then I lost my patience and told him the game was no fun unless he paid attention. Don apologized but added that the game wasn't much fun for him anyway. We decided not to play any more.

This was unfortunate, because it was one of the few things we could do together during the storms. Our conversations either died insipidly or led to arguments. I felt so frustrated by the weather that I had to get angry at something; Don was the nearest object and the only one capable of response.

The only events during the storm days that we could look forward to were meals. When we had finished one, we would set the time for the next, usually five or six hours later. Lunches we could spread out over the hours as we liked; but breakfasts and dinners had to be cooked. When the time arrived, one of us would curl up or sit up to make room for the stove. To compensate for this inconvenience, the other had to get the food and snow for the pots. When the wind was blowing, this could be a grim job: the fine snow shot inside the tent, and a hand scooping or groping outside would grow painfully numb. At last it got to be such a nuisance that we kept the food box inside all the time, even though it meant that it was hard to find room for our legs. The most comfortable position was to keep our legs slightly bent; but every now and then we had to straighten them. The ends of our sleeping bags were usually touching each other. If one of us felt his legs cramped, he began to think the other was taking up more than his share of space. It took the greatest restraint not to complain about it. When we eventually did, it took the form of aggravating politeness: "Do you have any more room down there?" "Could you move over just a little? My feet are against the wall." Gradually, for me at least—and I think for Don too—the nuisances encouraged a subtle defensiveness. I was always sure Don was more comfortable than I, sometimes at the expense of my own comfort. For instance, a few days earlier I had tried to broach a conversation about food—did we have enough, and did it seem enough, day by day? Don, I thought, had discouraged the talk. Now I began to look forward to meals inordinately; sometimes I daydreamed about food, simply to pass the time until the next meal, and I read sometimes only for the sake of filling up the same time. I tried not to look at the watch too often but couldn't help doing so eight or nine times a day. But Don seemed unaffected by these problems. Therefore I decided my hunger was only psychological, a function of boredom. So I kept quiet. We played a kind of gamesmanship when eating time neared (though I didn't realize until later that it was also gamesmanship for Don). Typically, our conversation would take this form:

"Don . . . it's about five-twenty."

"Hmm . . . what time did we say for dinner?"

"Five-thirty, I think."

"You hungry?"

"Well, not terribly. I could eat, though."

"That's about how I feel."

"Well, what do you think?"

"Just let me finish this short story first."

In the back of both our minds was the necessity of stretching the three meals over a full twenty-four hours. That was what made sleeping so attractive: the time passed fastest then. I remember waking several mornings, when my first thought was not *How is the weather?* but *Is it time for breakfast yet?*

Another nuisance of being tent-bound was that the inside of the tent gradually got wetter and wetter. Our breath would condense on the walls and sleeping bags, and the warmth of our bodies, even through the rubber pads, would cause small pools of water to form on the floor of the tent. We tried to sponge the walls and floor regularly, but we couldn't keep the bags dry. Gradually not only their covers, but the goose down inside grew damp, then wet; correspondingly, the bags kept us less warm. Often our feet or knees got cold. In normal weather we would have had enough sunshine to dry the bags out.

At last the storm exhausted itself. During the day of July 4, small patches of blue appeared among the clouds. We prepared to go that night. We were surprised to realize that it was already the fourth of July —in our predictions we had thought it possible to have reached the summit by then. Instead, we were three thousand feet below it and had not even begun the real climbing. I recalled last year's fourth of July, when we had sat in warm, clear weather outside a camp on McKinley, giving each other haircuts and already talking about reaching the summit in another week.

That night we set out. To the north, clouds boiled over the Gillam Glacier, the tops of them just below us. It was cold and crisp underfoot, but the dampness of our clothes and the long, logy hours in the tent made us get cold easily. We moved fast to try to warm up but never really succeeded. Our tracks had completely vanished. We had been counting on this; but we were alarmed when, on the far side of the ridge, we could find no trace of the aluminum stakes either. Everything looked the same, and we had only a vague memory of where we had placed the stakes. It would have been pointless to dig for them; it could have taken a week to find one.

We had counted pitches on the way up; now we counted them backwards, trying to hit the right altitude, always fearful, besides, of the hidden crevasses. The new snow seemed dangerous for avalanches as well.

At last I caught sight of a faint mark in the snow. When we approached, we saw with great relief that it was the upper two or three inches of the lowest aluminum stake. It was the only one left showing at all! I belayed from the stake while Don descended to try to find the highest fixed rope, buried somewhere just above the invisible ice cliff. He could only go to what seemed the top of the cliff, then dig in the snow with his axe. Thanks to his good memory, he found the rope fairly quickly. We descended the ice pitches rapidly, though even there the ropes were completely buried. Fortunately, the ice steps were still solid. Some of the ice-screw anchors had melted loose, but the long daggers were still frozen in.

We found the cache in good shape. We packed up some climbing equipment and three of the precious food boxes, good for twelve days. On the way back up we marked the route again and carefully measured the distance to the ridge.

At our high point, around 10,000 feet, we heard a soft whirring sound. We looked up in time to see a single, tiny bird flash by us. We were completely surprised; it was the first living thing we had seen for days, and it was even higher than the lichens on the rock seemed to grow.

As we descended to the col, the clouds that had been gathering below rose and engulfed us. In a few moments it was snowing again. The pattern was so familiar that we felt little disappointment; instead, as we crawled back into the comparative warmth of the tent, we felt relieved that we had been able to get the vital food boxes up before a new storm hit.

Until now the wind had been predominantly from the north. This time a strong gale from the south swept over the col, drifting the snow in a whole set of different places. Our protective snow wall did no good: it even seemed to help the drift collect. Our tent was the only object that stuck above the flat crest of the col, so the snow drifted easily around it anyway. At 2:30 P.M. the snow had reached a point halfway up the walls of the tent. Don went outside and thoroughly shoveled away the drift. We were alarmed when, only four hours later, the drift had reached the previous level. This time I went out. It took more than an hour to dig out the tent. As the blinding wind, filled with snow, roared across the ridge, I had the feeling of being lost in a desert. I couldn't even glimpse Deborah. All that existed were the tent, the snow, and the shovel.

Four hours later we had to do the job again. We had never seen snow like this, that could drift so quickly. It was making what should have been a rest day hard work. One of us would have to stay awake now, watching the dark snowline slowly rise on the side of the tent.

At 2:30 A.M. we finished the third shoveling job. We were both tired and sleepy. We settled in again to wait. The monotonous roar of the wind was hypnotic, and it was almost dark inside.

Apparently, we both fell asleep. When I awoke, I was aware of the wall of the tent sagging heavily about an inch from my face. It was almost pitch dark inside and strangely quiet. I tried to force myself to be alert, but I felt a strong desire to fall asleep again. Looking up, I could see only a thin strip of light, just along the ridge pole, at the top of the tent.

Instantly I realized what had happened. "Don!" I said, "Wake up!" The air seemed to be stale and stuffy. I tried to sit up, but the wall got in my way. Eeriest of all was the quiet. Don awoke. "We're almost buried," I said urgently. I managed to reach Don's watch. It was 9:30 A.M., seven hours after our last shoveling.

Don offered to get dressed. Only one of us could move at a time. Awkwardly, he pulled on his pants and boots. Then he slid out of his bag. He started pounding the door of the tent back, at first with his hands, then with his shoulder in lunges, like the football lineman he had been in high school. With intense relief we saw that the snow gave behind the door, though it did not fall away.

At last Don had enough room to open the door. Snow fell in at once when he did, but I grabbed the door behind him as he slithered out. He managed to fight his way up and out of the little trench he had formed. I could barely hear him swear as he got out; later he described to me the frightening sight of a smooth, wind-lashed plain of snow, out of which protruded only an orange, horizontal pole. Had the snow covered that last bit, we might never have awakened.

We had carefully placed the shovel, and Don found it quickly. With a vengeance he dug away the drift. It took hours. As he gradually uncovered the tent, he saw that the strong poles had been bent out of shape by the weight of the snow.

Before he got the tent completely dug out, Don decided that the only thing to do was to move the tent. I agreed with him and got dressed to go out and help him. The wind was blowing bitterly, but we managed to pull the tent loose. We had left everything inside it, to make it simple to move. We climbed out of the hole we had been in, pulled the tent out, and repitched it nearby.

The move seemed a great improvement, for we had only a minor drifting problem after that. We were still tired from the exertion: contrary to our usual feeling during storms, we wanted to rest instead of to get moving. In the evening I had to go out, first for a bowel movement and second, to get a new food box. I dreaded the first task. The wind had slackened not at all. I dashed out during a lull that was gone immediately and walked a distance from the tent. I pulled my pants down quickly and squatted. It was utterly miserable: the blowing snow got inside my pants and blew up under my shirt. Shivering, I pulled up my pants.

Now I had to find the pile of supplies, which was totally buried. Fortunately, we had been careful to locate it to the exact foot with respect to the tent. We had moved the tent, but its hole, rapidly filling with snow, was still visible. I started digging. It was hard work but warmed me up. Astonishingly, I got to the food box only when I was seven or eight feet down, having dug a pit deeper than my height. That much snow had drifted there in less than two days! I pulled a food box out and returned, very tired and wet, to the tent. Later Don went out and moved the whole pile of supplies, putting them nearer the tent, stacked tighter.

Before the drifting problem we had had trouble with the radio. It had broadcast all right, but we had had difficulty understanding what Fairbanks was saying. We had assumed it was weather interference because the radio had worked so well on the 2nd. Now, in our new site, we tried the radio again. This time neither the broadcasting nor the receiving worked well. We were quite upset; it couldn't be the battery, for we had a spare one that worked no better. We had been so careful of the damned thing: I had always carried it in the safest, softest spot in my pack; we had kept it absolutely dry, and we had warmed the batteries in our sleeping bags each time before trying the radio. Now it looked as if our only link with the outside world was cut off.

We lay in apathetic discouragement. The hunger was as strong as ever. At last we had admitted to each other that we *were* hungry. But we could not understand why; we thought we had enough calories and vitamins, especially for the storm days, when we usually did little work. Perhaps, Don suggested, we burned a lot of calories simply trying to keep warm in our soggy sleeping bags. Perhaps, I ventured, it was purely psychological but was affecting both of us. Whatever the cause, we definitely felt hungry. For a short while we sensed a friendly cooperation, partly because we had acknowledged the hunger, partly because of the close escape in the tent.

But it wore off. Our chances on Deborah seemed almost vanished. We had, stretching it, at most fourteen days' food left on the col. Our only hope was good weather and a dash for the summit. But we knew the route was too difficult for dashing. Still, there was always a chance. We developed a defensive feeling of pride. As I had written in my diary as early as the fourth, "We like to think others would have quit by now."

I had been having wish-fulfillment dreams. Typically, I would be a guest at a buffet dinner where every imaginable delicacy was heaped in inexhaustible piles on a huge table. There would be scores of other guests, people to talk to, all my home and Harvard friends, surrounding me. Don, though, was never there. But each time, as I started to eat, someone would interrupt me with a question. . . . Finally I would wake up and see the dull crisscross pattern of the orange tent wall above my face and know that nothing had changed, that it was still three hours until dinner.

I developed another problem, apparently related to the humidity. Even though we weren't drinking very much, I had to urinate every three or four hours. If I was asleep, I would dream about an indoor bathroom in some house to which I could pad, barefoot, in my pajamas. But something would always hinder me: perhaps I couldn't lift the seat to the toilet. . . . At last I would wake up, pull on my pants and boots, and dash out into the storm. I dreaded it, and having to do it every few hours seemed a terrible burden. I thought of an alternative. I would take a used plastic bag from our food box, urinate into it, tie off the top, then throw it out the door. Don didn't like the idea but bore it silently two or three times. He was worried about the bag leaking; so I agreed to place my eating bowl under it.

The process, disgusting as it would have seemed to me otherwise, was much more pleasant than going outside. But Don got fed up. He argued with me that it was an emergency procedure and that it was dangerous to resort to it before we were in a real emergency. Besides, he noticed the faint smell of urine in the air for a long time afterward, and the smell nauseated him slightly. After this complaint, I agreed not to use the plastic bags any more.

The weather improved the evening of July 7. We set

out at 9:30 P.M. for the last trip back to the cache. In the northwest, the sun was setting in a purple blaze of clouds. As I stopped to take a picture of it, I dropped a mitten. We watched it roll lazily away; three hundred feet below us, it stopped on a snow ledge. Don wanted to go on, but I insisted on retrieving it. Restraining his annoyance, Don climbed down with me, giving me a belay on the last part so that I could reach the mitten. We wasted forty-five minutes on this delay and much-needed energy.

When we got off the ridge to the south, we found a wind-slab crust everywhere. It looked extremely likely to avalanche. But there was no way to avoid it, and no anchor to place to make it safer. If an avalanche had broken off, we couldn't have stayed out of it, and it would have carried us three thousand feet, certainly to our deaths. Moreover, there was a danger that our line of tracks itself might cut off a slab of snow and start an avalanche. Accordingly, we tried to take big steps and avoided long horizontal traverses as much as possible.

Again the marking stakes were buried. Our careful measurements paid off though; we recognized lumps of snow and subtle contours and found the vicinity of the ice cliff. Then, just as before, we saw a few inches of the lowest stake protruding above the snow. This time the stake marked the top of the fixed rope itself.

Once more we found the ice steps covered with snow but still solid. We went briskly down the pitches, counting the hard part of the job done. But as we rounded the last corner above the cache, we saw no sign of it.

When we got to where the cache should have been, we could see that an avalanche had covered everything, even the identifying rocks just below it. For all we knew, our supplies had been swept away.

We tried to reorient, measuring our distance down from the lowest ice screw. There was nothing to do but probe with our ice-axe shafts for the cache. For a long time we had no luck. Here and there our probes hit rock, which meant that the snow wasn't deeper than the length of our axes. But it seemed hopeless. At last, as we were about to give up, I tried farther to the right and hit something soft. It was the last food box. Thanks to the piton, the whole cache had held. Relieved, we dug it out and packed it up.

As we climbed the ice cliff for the last time, we pulled out the fixed ropes. We would need them on the route itself, later. The screws came out easily, but the aluminum daggers were frozen in so solidly that we broke them off trying to get them out.

We dashed across the wind-slab slope, glad to be over it for the last time, and descended wearily to the col.

The inevitable storm arrived. We stayed put all the next day and the next night as well, sleeping and thinking about food. The wind was coming from a new direction, the southwest, but we had less of a drifting problem than before. Our hunger seemed to have increased in the last few days, perhaps because we had talked about it. We had devised a system for dividing the meal into equal halves, at first only for the sake of impartiality. The rule was that the one who divided the portion gave up the choice to the other. To even things out, each of us had to divide different items. But at breakfast, for instance, there were only three things that needed splitting; hence one of us had to split two of them. To make this fair, we exchanged jobs each day. This complicated system would have been absurd normally; but we watched each other distrustfully, and when we had to cut a piece of Logan bread or pour cereal out of a bag, we did so with painstaking care. At first we covered the ritual with nonchalance. Don would finish dividing and say, "O.K., take your pick. Which one looks bigger?"

I would answer, "I can't tell, they look about the same."

"Couldn't be much difference either way."

Reaching for the portion I had in my mind carefully weighed and found heavier, I would say, "I'll just take this one; it looks fine."

We tried to eat slowly, making the meal last. But when it was done, we were still hungry. Cramped in our bags, we would curl up and try to sleep; if sleep wouldn't come, we would reach for a damp paperback book, open it, and try to concentrate on the irrelevant words.

8 ▲

The weather cleared at noon on the 9th. By that evening, amazingly enough, it was still clear. Eagerly, we got dressed to go; for the first time we would head toward Deborah, not away from it. We put on our canvas-soled overboots for extra warmth and strapped our crampons beneath them.

As Don led away from the tent, I felt a momentary thrill. It was like starting all over; every inch of ground was new again. As we neared Deborah, the flat platform we were on gradually narrowed, becoming first a broad ridge and finally a knife-edge of snow. As the ridge got narrower and we became increasingly aware of the sheer drop on either side, I had the feeling of walking out on a gangplank. For the last six rope-lengths, we belayed each other. It was not difficult going, but it was certainly spectacular. At places, we had only about a foot's width of safe snow: on the left we could see the cracks where avalanches had broken off and plunged to the floor of the West Fork Glacier; on the right, the tricky cornice overhung empty air and the Gillam Glacier. The belayer vaguely intended, if the leader fell off one side, to jump off the other. It might work as a last resort, though we weren't sure how to get back to the ridge after such a thing might happen. Fortunately, the snow was solid, and we had no troubles. All the same, we had to go slowly; inevitably the belayer got very cold as he stood in his steps, managing the rope.

We had crossed the knife-edge and reached the first rock cliff by midnight. As I hammered the first piton into a crack, I was dismayed to see the rock break away and crumble. It was fully as rotten as the stuff we had found on the way up to the ice cliff. By now we had expected this, but it proved discouraging anyway. We stood together, shivering, on the ledge just below the cliff. The first part of it was steeper than vertical. The rock was clearly difficult enough so that we might have to take off our overboots and, in places, our mittens. Somehow, in the cold, we could not bring ourselves to do it. We realized that if we were going to climb at all, it would have to be during the daytime, bad snow conditions or not. It was simply too cold at night; the cold itself made our climbing dangerous.

We left our supplies hanging from the piton I had hammered in, then returned to camp. We got back only four hours after we had left, feeling slightly annoyed that we hadn't been able to use more of our clear weather. But we knew we had made the right decision.

We planned to sleep briefly, then try to climb in the daytime. True to the familiar pattern, the skies clouded, the wind sprang up from the north, and it began to snow. We were pleased to have, if ever so slightly, started the route. But in the backs of our minds we already knew we were probably defeated. Still, we did not admit it to each other: we talked of "pushing" and of getting a break in the weather. But I wrote in my diary that morning, "At least we will be able to say we made a good try."

The treacherous snow began to drift against the tent in much the same way that it had when we were nearly buried. Don dug it out once; after that, the snow rapidly piled up to the midpoint of the walls, but it seemed to stabilize there. Uneasily, we started to relax. But it got warm during the day, and the drifted snow started to melt through the walls. We realized the only thing to do was to move the tent again. I dug it loose; then Don joined me to pull the tent to the other side of the supplies, where we repitched it at a slightly different angle. For some reason, which we were too grateful for to bother figuring out, the drifting problem vanished.

We took the back off the radio to try to figure out

what was wrong with it. What we found was an immensely complicated circuit of transistors. With very little mechanical aptitude, I couldn't hope to figure it out; Don, irked by my lack of patience, studied the diagram carefully and tried to check the connections. Our hands, cold and clumsy, couldn't handle the tiny parts very well. At one point, one of us broke a wire. I was ready to give up completely, but Don patiently figured out where it belonged and managed to reattach it. We put the thing back together, then tried broadcasting. The radio was virtually dead. When we tried to receive, we could only get faint static.

We slept listlessly. The storm continued without change; by now we were so accustomed to its sound that we might have felt uneasy in the silence of a clear day. In the middle of the night, while I was asleep, Don heard a different sound, a deeper rumble, and felt the tent shake. In a few moments it was over. It was so gentle that I didn't wake up, but Don thought it was probably an earthquake. After all, it had been only four months since the disastrous quake in Anchorage. Was this another hazard we were going to have to worry about? Suppose we were climbing on the rock wall when an earthquake hit—would it shake us off?

The strain we were feeling was subtle and undermining. We felt physically relaxed most of the time; so much so, that if the weather showed even a hint of improving, we began to feel guilty for not climbing. But for all our leisure, we were undergoing an enervating change. The food was most important; though we couldn't be sure of it, we were losing weight steadily. We thought about food even when we thought we were thinking about something else. A dozen times I told myself what fools we had been not to throw in a huge sack of oatmeal—it would have cost so little. Had the radio worked, we might conceivably have been able to call our pilot, Warbelow, asking him to drop some extra food to us on the col. But that was out of the question now. In our diaries, both of us began unconsciously to transfer the adjectives of enthusiasm— "wonderful," "beautiful," "great"—from the mountain and the scenery to our meals.

We had partly dropped the habit of arguing; we knew that we would get too angry at each other, regardless of the pretext. We tended to withdraw into ourselves, and our dreams began to use up the supply of imagination that we might once have shared in a good talk. My "banquet" dreams became more frequent and more believable; my "bathroom" dreams, more elaborate and fantastic. Don noticed a tendency in his own dreams away from the mountains, toward the familiar past of his home and friends; but always, he noted in his diary, with "some terrible new element—a combination of the nostalgic and the grotesque."

Outwardly, things were calm between us. But I felt the lack of communication poignantly. I had got into the habit of reacting to Don's mannerisms—to the way he cleaned his knife, or held his book, or even breathed. The temptation was to invent rationalizations: I told myself that I got mad at his deliberate way of spooning up his breakfast cereal because it was indicative of his methodicalness, which was indicative of a mental slowness, which was why he disliked and opposed my impatience. The chain of rationalizations almost always resulted, thus, in a defensive feeling; I was becoming, in the stagnation of our situation, both aggressive and paranoid. So I would try to keep from thinking about it; instead I would daydream about the pleasures of warmer, easier living. But all the while I could be working myself into a silent rage over the sound of Don's chewing as he ate a candy bar.

We had a brief flare-up on the 11th when Don decided to clean the stove at the precise time we had set for breakfast. Though I didn't say so, I suspected that Don had planned the cleaning simply to delay breakfast, which, he might think, would make it easier to wait for lunch. He probably felt indignant, in turn, at the fact that I wouldn't even bother with such things as cleaning the stove unless he suggested it.

For once the argument took a positive twist and evolved into a discussion about the future. In particular, we talked about the possibility that our second airdrop, over by Mount Hayes, had been lost under the nearly incessant snowfall of the last few weeks. We both imagined getting to the airdrop site, low on food, only to see a smooth, snow-covered basin. And we talked about the possibility of failure on Deborah. I remembered the first days, now more than a week past, that I had entertained the thought; it had seemed impossible, somehow beneath us, to fail. Now I was quite sure of it. But Don was unwilling to give up, and his attitude gave me a germ of new hope: if only we could get some good weather.

On the morning of the 12th, I looked out the tent door to see a pale mist, beneath which ominous clouds billowed in the north. But the wind had almost stopped blowing. We decided to give it a try, and would have been off by 4:00 A.M., except that Don discovered that a trickle of water had rolled off the tent wall and into his boots, where it had frozen to ice. We had to spend an extra two and a half hours thawing the ice over the stove. I was furiously impatient and even suggested, though I knew better, that Don should put on his boots, ice or no ice, so that we could get off. As in all our outbursts, dozens of other hostilities reached the surface; but, as in all our recent arguments, the bitter words had an important function for us as release. They allowed us to puncture what Don called the "sound barrier"— the hours of wordless antagonism when our nerves wound tighter and tighter. By the time Don's boots were dry, we felt friendly again—painfully friendly, like lovers after a quarrel. Our situation was, of course, something like that of lovers or married people, except that, instead of a bond of physical love, our bond was danger and the mountain. But our relationship was importantly different too. Frustratingly, we could not conciliate like lovers; we had to express our feelings in self-conscious terms that denied the real affection we felt for each other, in talk of "getting along" and "climbing well together." Thus, after all our arguments, a sense of embarrassment lingered with us, a desire to "make up," for which we could not find the right words.

We got moving by 6:30 A.M. At once, it looked as if the shape of the ridge had changed drastically. We attributed it at first to a confusion of memory, since our previous steps had been covered by snow. But Don thought of the possibility that the earthquake in the night had shifted the ridge slightly or broken off sections of it. A few days later our old steps miraculously reappeared, and we saw them lead right off the present edge of the ridge into space, rejoining the ridge a few hundred yards farther on. What would an airplane pilot flying over have made of that line of steps! It was an idle speculation: we had not seen an airplane since the first day of the expedition.

We reached the first rock cliff by 8:15 A.M. Though we had been going less than two hours, we decided to eat half our lunch there. At least there was a small platform of snow to sit on, and the cliff gave us some shelter. We each ate a candy bar, a few bites of dried sausage, and a lemon candy or two. The air felt warm, although a light, wet snow was falling. We took off our crampons and overboots so that the rubber soles of our boots could touch the rock. After lunch I started the first pitch as Don belayed me from our little platform. Rounding a corner to the left, I entered a steep chute of snow. Out of sight of Don, I soon found myself shoveling piles of snow away to get to the rock underneath. How absurd it seemed to be burrowing in the snow like a gopher, on the side of this mountain, which no one but us had ever really seen, much less cared about; to go short on food and patience simply to be allowed to paw through the snow in search of rock! But I was excited and happy; at last we were back to real climbing. With a foot on either side of the chute, gradually I could work my way up it. After a long time I was standing directly above Don, at the top of the little overhang that protected him. I shouted, and we flipped the rope out of the chute so that it ran straight up to me. I moved up for sixty feet more, hammering an almost worthless piton for "safety" at the hardest point and two more pitons for an anchor above. Don came up; he had been getting cold, standing there—now it was my turn to shiver. The rock above was even more rotten than what I had found on my lead—almost like frozen, chunky mud. But Don slowly and carefully worked his way up the last thirty feet. At last he was at the top of the cliff. He found an anchor and brought me up. We complimented each other for two and a half hours of work that had got us up a paltry 140 feet of the mountain. Still, it was as hard as anything we had done on McKinley the year before, and our fingers were still tingling with the feel of the rock. We ate the rest of our lunches. It was almost noon; we kept thinking about the knife-edged snow ridge softening in the warmth of the day. We had to go back. We stretched a single fixed rope all the way down to the snow platform. As we hurried back over the sharp ridge, we saw to the south, all along the massive wall of Deborah, little avalanches shooting downward, one or two each minute. By the time we got back to the tent we were tired and famished. Dinner was a bland "glop" of powdered egg and rice—but it had become our favorite because it was the largest.

The weather seemed to be getting steadily nicer. By now we knew better than to count on anything lasting, but we looked forward to whatever chance of working on the route we might get. There was still a faint hope for the summit. One rope-length for a day's work—it didn't seem much at all. But in good weather we would go much farther. Still, we had been tired when we got back, very tired. Perhaps it was all those days of inactivity; perhaps it was the lack of food. One thing was clear: we would soon need a new camp site on the ridge. It took too long to retrace all the old steps each day, and the farther we got, the more there would be to retrace. So far, however, we had hardly found a place where we could sit down, much less pitch a tent.

But we went to bed happy and slept soundly that night.

At 1:30 A.M. Don woke up to go outside. The mist had cleared completely; the crisp, startling blue of clear sky surrounded us. In the northeast the sun was just rising. It looked like the best day we had had in weeks. Don photographed the sunrise, trying to shake off the aura of a nightmare he had been having. In it someone, some close friend of his, had died or been in a violent accident; it was all fuzzy, elusive, disturbing.

We got started by 5:00 A.M. This time we attached

our crampons directly to our boots, leaving off the overboots. The snow was in fine shape, frozen and crunchy.
We moved together, without belaying, and nearly flew
across the knife-edge. Exuberantly, we knew that we
were working together as well as was possible. The
fixed rope helped immensely on the rock cliff. In only an
hour and a half we were as high as we had got the day
before. Quickly we climbed three pitches of steep and
somewhat treacherous snow, warily staying below the
cornices. Twice we hammered the aluminum daggers
that Don had made into the soft slope for protection;
even they seemed not to hold very well, but they gave
us some psychological security. To belay, we would
stamp down a little pocket of snow, thrust the axe as
far in as possible, then feed the rope around the head
of the axe. Often we could sit down, which made the
belaying much more comfortable. Still, there were no
level spots, or even gentle ones, and certainly no places
to pitch a tent.

As I belayed, facing outward, I saw a huge white
mountain far in the distance to the southeast. We figured out that it was Mount Sanford, some 140 miles
away. The air was so splendidly clear that we fancied
we could see rivers meandering in the lowlands to the
south. It was the first day of the whole expedition that
we had been at a high altitude on a clear day. We could
estimate in the gray-blue flatness where the road was
that we had hiked in from twenty-five days before.

At the top of the third pitch I reached an isolated
block of rock. Curiously, it was far more solid than any

of the rock below; the piton rang in the cold air as I hammered it in. On the next pitch, while Don climbed out of sight above, I felt wonderfully secure. Again the route grew difficult. Don had to scramble up patches of rock and snow until he reached a prong of rock, on the north side of which he swung around. As he did so, he was dizzily hanging over the vertical drop above the Gillam, which we had never been able to look down before on account of the cornices. After this, he climbed over a tower that was topped with a froth of snow, like whipped cream, through which he dug a kind of canal. On the tower's far side he had to drop into a deep gap spanned by unstable snow, from which he clambered onto rock. I yelled that he was out of rope. He went a little farther and hammered in a mediocre piton. This was exciting stuff! Nothing on McKinley had been so spectacular. Don's pitch had been the hardest yet, and it was still early in the day.

I climbed above, finishing the short, tricky cliff and forging up a smooth snow slope to a big rock. When Don came up, we stopped for lunch. For once we didn't mind the meager amount of food. We were full of optimism and spoke almost breathlessly about our progress. It looked easier above. As we ate, we craned our necks back to try to gauge how high we were on the mountain. We knew the steepest part of the ridge was yet to come, a frightening, nearly vertical 600-foot wall of rotten black rock. And above that was a thousand feet of steep ridge, festooned with the unbelievable curls, loops, and blossoms of ice we had seen from our tent. But it looked easier just above us, and our hearts leaped. For once we hurried through the lunch instead of trying to make it last. The sun was warm enough for comfort. This was what we had come to Alaska for!

Above, we had to go carefully, for the snow thinned in places to a bare skin over the ice beneath. Long sections of steps had to be chopped with the ice axe. The higher we got, the more empty space seemed to yawn below us. So far there had not been a single spot on the whole route where, had we fallen, we should have had a chance of stopping before the floor of the glacier, three thousand feet below. But to prevent that was what the rope, the pitons, the ice daggers, and all our skill were for.

Alternating leads, we climbed three quick pitches. At the top of a fourth, I reached rock again. We were tempted to go on but knew it was time to return; it was past noon, and the snow was melting. On the way down we were forced to go slowly, often having to improve the sun-weakened steps. We hadn't carried enough rope with us to string over all the route, but we placed fixed lines on the lowest five pitches.

As we neared the bottom we grew extremely tired. The snow on the knife-edge was very dangerous; much as we wanted to hurry over it, we had to go slowly, with gingerly steps. At last, at 5:00 P.M., we stumbled back to the tent, near exhaustion after twelve hours of hard climbing. Our throats were parched for lack of water, but we were tremendously happy. True, we had found no reasonable camp site yet, but the weather seemed to be getting even better; indeed, this was the first entirely clear day of the whole expedition. And we had done nine new pitches in a single day!

In the tent, we were overjoyed to find our sleeping bags drier than they had been in weeks. Lying down seemed a luxury again. We talked about whether or not we could keep up such a pace and whether such a pace might make the summit possible. Despite our enthusiasm, we really knew how unlikely success was. We had only about a week's food left on the col; with any safety margin at all, we could afford to climb, at most, three or four more days. We needed at least a day's food to get down to base camp, and a storm might besiege us at any time. But it wasn't in our hearts to waste such good weather.

From the best picture we had had, months before, we had hypothesized a camp site on a short, apparently level gap of ridge at 10,400 feet. We guessed that we had got almost that high already. Perhaps in the next effort we could reach the gap. If a camp could be placed there, then the following day we might move the tent, or Don's tiny bivouac tent, up there. And then, the day after, dash for the summit? But a "dash" over the hardest two thousand feet of the climb was out of the question. Still, with some unforeseeable break . . .

But the effort was hard on us. We fell asleep right after dinner, knowing that all too soon it would be morning again and that we would *have* to get an early start for the sake of good snow conditions. We almost wished for a storm, simply to rest. Best of all, though, with the good weather there had been hardly an ill word between us. That night we slept as sound as rocks —sounder, in fact, than the rocks on Deborah.

July 14 dawned even clearer than the day before. We got started at 6:10 A.M., impatient but still tired from the day before. When we reached the first cliff we decided, for the sake of speed, not to take off our crampons. This worked surprisingly well: the spikes held on the crumbly, wet rock at least as well as the rubber soles of our boots had. Above the cliff, we found the snow in splendid shape; in places our steps were like plaster casts. The cold nights, without precipitation, had allowed the snow to freeze hard. Don suggested that we climb continuously, a rope-length apart, without belaying. It was pretty difficult climbing not to belay, but we tried it. It worked perfectly; our instinctive understanding of each other, even when we were out of sight, paid off now. We were making remarkable speed. I felt a piercing joy—Don was the only one in the world with whom I could have climbed like this; in fact, there were few people anywhere who could do this as capably as we. If we did no more climbing the whole trip, we could remember this day with gratitude.

In the astonishingly short time of one hour and forty minutes from the tent, we had reached our previous high point. I led on. The little rock cliff was no trouble, but the snow above it suddenly changed in character from the solid stuff below. On a very steep, wrinkled slope, I traversed to the left. I had to climb almost on the cornice, and I prayed that it would hold. A powdery surface layer of snow brushed off at the touch; underneath, instead of firm snow or hard ice, I found a pocked and brittle lacework of ice, like a hideous honeycomb, that seemed limitlessly deep. The whole ridge was made more out of air than anything else. I placed an ice screw that seemed to offer a little security; when Don followed later, though, he picked it out of the slope with his fingers. The farther I got above Don, the more I felt as if I were walking on a kind of cloud that might suddenly collapse. Finally I put in a dagger, which, though it wouldn't have held a long fall, seemed better than nothing. If not the most difficult, this was the scariest pitch yet. When Don came up, we were suddenly isolated from the rock, with nothing but the honeycomb holding us to the mountain. But there was rock about forty feet above us; with infinite caution, Don led beyond me. For a little while the slope got very steep. I think I was holding my breath as I belayed. At last Don reached the rock where, after some searching, he could hammer in a piton. At once I felt better. Don found an ample, but narrow and downsloping, ledge from which to belay me. There we had half a lunch, a few minutes after 10:00 A.M. We were less than a pitch below the sharp plume that hid the level gap— our hoped-for camp site.

After we had eaten, I led on. Don had a fairly good rock piton for anchor. As I climbed the plume, it got steeper and steeper and smaller and smaller. Halfway up, I stuck my axe through the cornice into blank air on the right side. A few minutes later I did the same on the left side. This was appalling; the plume was corniced on both sides! I tried to hug the middle and ended up virtually crawling up it, almost like shinnying up a pole of horrible, empty, airy ice. Still, I was dying with curiosity to see over the top. A long stake I tried to place for protection went in and out like a toothpick in butter. Clumsily, but carefully, I inched to the top, then looked over.

In a glance that lasted a few moments, the expedition seemed to end. I stood silent, not quite able to believe what I saw. Both Don and I had thought about the little gap often, and it must have taken on in our imaginations something of the quality of a heavenly oasis. Perhaps we had even begun to think of it as a reward in itself, like the summit, an isle of safety in the middle of a vertical sea of danger. At best it would be a broad, flat platform, as big as a tennis court; if things went badly, perhaps only the size of a large mattress. But we could pitch a tent on a mattress.

What I saw, instead, was a serpentine wisp of snow, like the curl of a ribbon on edge. This time I could see the double cornice—the whole of the little bridge was undercut incredibly on both sides, so that it looked as if a strong wind might topple it. It was only ten feet below me and thirty feet long. The last ten feet of it were impossibly thin. Next, I saw the face of the mountain beyond. The crumbly brown rock towered, flat and crackless, a few degrees less than vertical. A thin, splotchy coating of ice overlay most of the rock. Where the rock overhung, great icicles grew. A few vertical columns of plastered snow, like frozen snakes, stuck to the coating of ice. And above, blocking out half the sky, was the terrible black cliff, the six-hundred-foot wall that we had once blithely, back in Cambridge, allowed three days to climb. At its upper rim, nearly a thousand feet above me, hovered monstrous chunks of ice, like aimed cannons at the top of a castle wall. As I watched, one broke off, fell most of the six hundred feet without touching anything, then smashed violently on a ledge to my left and bounced out of sight down the precipice.

I had never seen a mountain sight so numbing, so haunted with impossibility and danger. Don yelled up, "How does it look?" I almost laughed. I shouted back something inane, like "Not so good." Then I told Don that I would climb just over the plume to try to find a spot from which to bring him up. I pivoted over the top and started kicking steps down the back side of the little tower. Bizarrely, I felt safer at once, because the rope passed over the plume; if I fell, it might conceivably act like a piton. My feet broke through the steps, and I half slid down to the bridge. I walked out a few feet on it, just short of the point where it grew impossibly narrow. Then I tried to stand in the middle of the little gap, as I delicately stamped the snow down under my feet. It gave and gave; soon I was nearly shoulder deep in it. I could imagine myself imbedded in the ice-cream cone as the whole thing toppled off its pedestal. There was something desperately ludicrous about it. My axe could find nothing that gave any resistance. But it was safer than being on the other side of the plume when Don came up.

I yelled, "Off belay!" Don had trouble hearing me

and yelled back something indistinguishable. His voice seemed infinitely remote. At last we communicated by rope tuggings; then, as I gradually pulled in the rope, I could tell he was slowly climbing.

Don's head poked over the top of the plume. "Don't come any farther," I said. "It isn't safe." Don stood there, as transfixed as I had been; perhaps more so, for he saw me sitting like a pilot in a plunging airplane, in the cockpit of the bridge of snow. As he looked, the inevitable decision, without a word, passed between us. We could go no farther; Deborah's summit was unattainable. With another twenty days' food and some kind of equipment not yet invented and brazen skill, perhaps we could have gone on. With a handful of days left, a few puny fixed ropes, a few pitons made for rock that stayed in one piece, and some vestiges of sanity, we had to give up.

Of course we were sad. But as we turned to head down, we were almost lighthearted, too. The mountain had been fair to us; it had unequivocally said *Stop*, instead of leading us seductively on and on, forcing the decision of failure on us, so that we might suspect and blame only our weaknesses. The mountain had allowed us pride.

9 ▲

The descent was dangerous. The snow had melted to the point of sloppiness. We had to go slowly, but the longer we took, the longer the hot sun had to attack the snow. Near the bottom we grew tired again. Don was going first; each of our steps he methodically tried to reinforce or kick deeper. I got impatient and fumed silently. At last I said, "Can't you go a little faster?" He turned on me with angry words, telling me I should be aware of how bad the snow conditions were. His point was soon proved; twice my steps broke out under me, and I started sliding down the steep slope. Each time, I tried to dig the point of my axe in as a brake, but it took the fixed rope, which I held in my left hand, to stop me. The second time, the force of my fall pulled out one of the daggers to which the rope was attached; fortunately, the rope was anchored elsewhere and held. All the same, these were frightening experiences for both of us. Much as I hated to, I mumbled some kind of apology to Don for having hurried him. We got back to camp at 4:30 P.M. and threw down our packs; for the third day in a row we were near exhaustion. But we began to cheer up with dinner. Afterwards, we had a few sips of our misnamed "victory brandy"—Don suggested calling it "consolation brandy."

A curious sense of peace surrounded our next few days. We were discouraged, but our failure had only clinched suspicions that had been growing in us, unuttered, for weeks. On the whole, the defeat tended to banish anxieties rather than produce them. We talked about our effort in detail; as always, in the last few days, the talking put us at ease instead of on edge. We had no energy left for loud arguments.

The weather showed no signs of worsening. Oh, what we might have done with such a spell of perfect days earlier! But our minds kept returning to the unforgettable picture of the little gap of snow, the stark, active wall above—the Nemesis, as we had nicknamed it—and we wondered if anyone would ever climb our route.

We could afford two or three more days on the col. We might have spent them trying the Nemesis; but we could not imagine a more futile project. Instead, we decided to climb the unnamed peak to the east of us, the summit we had passed under getting to the col. It looked like an easy day's climb, up a gently inclining ridge with no rock on it at all. After Deborah, it would be a picnic. And, besides it was unclimbed: Mount Hess, a mile northeast of it, had been ascended once, more than a decade before, but no one had touched this peak, which was simply marked "11,780" on the map.

We had decided to double our rations temporarily, since we could no longer use them on the route. The next morning, July 15, we had our first double breakfast: it was a marvelous luxury. We were a little worried that it would be hard, after splurging, to get back to our inadequate daily supply, but we couldn't bring ourselves to push asceticism so far as to deny ourselves now. Surprisingly, though, we did not feel stuffed after we had eaten, even with the double meal. Perhaps our extreme exertions in the last three days had burned a huge number of calories.

We made a late start, around 8:00 A.M. The weather was still perfectly clear and windless. Everything seemed so easy by comparison with our recent climbing. At about 10,200 feet we stopped to take pictures and decided to unrope. But as Don was walking across the platform of snow, camera in hand, he fell into a hidden crevasse. Fortunately, he went only about fifteen feet in. I threw down the rope, and he climbed out by himself. He was worried most about the camera having gotten wet. We were chastened, though; if crevasses could be found even on the crest of a ridge, they could be found anywhere. We resolved not to unrope again on any terrain.

For a next few hours we carefully crossed several other hidden crevasses and imagined a dozen others. The climb was just varied enough to be interesting. It reminded me of the White Mountains in New Hampshire, or of Colorado, and I dwelt briefly on memories of climbing there, picturing other friends whom I poignantly missed now. Don was leading, just before noon, as we came to the summit ridge. I watched him climb the last bit of hard snow and step to the top. Immediately, he shouted about the view. I came up as quickly as I could.

The whole panorama of the Hayes Range had opened before us. Don had seen it once before, from the airplane, but I was looking at it for the first time. Biggest of all was Mount Hayes, stretching its massive white arms to the north and the south. Beyond it, in the eastern distance, we could glimpse the tops of the high peaks that stood at the far end of the range. Glaciers wove shining in and out of chains of unclimbed, unknown mountains. For the first time, fifteen miles away, I could see the basin where we had dropped our second load of supplies. Low clouds hugged the surface of the glacier, but the sharp peaks we intended to climb poked their heads above. None of them would make up for Deborah, but they would help. They were other, easier challenges; perhaps we could partly forget our failure among them. Twenty-eight days of food, too—we could almost taste it already. Still, we wondered about the storms. The glaciers and walls looked unusually snowy for this late in the summer. Would we be able to find that parachute?

It was only a short walk to the top. We felt relaxed and exuberant as we strolled across the nearly level ridge. A few feet short of the summit I gave us both a scare by falling up to my shoulders in a crevasse. They were everywhere! We carefully belayed the last stretch. The summit itself appeared to be a cornice; hence only one of us at a time stood on it. We left one of our aluminum stakes to mark our ascent, though we knew the snows of winter would quickly cover it. Then we retreated a few yards, sat down, and ate a double lunch.

This was the highest point we had reached on the expedition; the highest, in fact, we were going to reach. We sat close to each other, in almost total comfort; I remember reflecting that it was remarkable, after nearly thirty days together, that we could have even a moment of such perfect friendship. I looked at Don. His shaggy, black beard covered most of his face; what I could see of his skin was deeply tanned, despite all our days of storm. But his face looked thin, too, and there were marks of strain about his eyes. I wondered how much he had changed; I could not really remember what he had looked like before. I wondered if my face looked different, too, and if I had really lost any weight.

On the way down, we stopped just before we passed into Deborah's shadow to eat the last scraps of our lunches. As we were sitting there we heard a strange sound in the air, then recognized it as that of a plane. All at once a small Air Force jet, with red markings, soared over. It made a sweeping circle low over Deborah, then flew off. Had it seen our tracks? Or was the shape of Deborah intriguing enough in itself? The plane had made no sign of noticing us. We watched it disappear without regret.

We were back to our tent by 4:00 P.M. We tried the radio once more, thinking the weather might have made some difference; but it was completely dead. Inside the tent we cooked our double dinner at once, as we talked about getting our money back on the radio rental after the trip. We would have liked to throw the thing off a cliff, but it was too valuable; we would have to carry its six pounds of useless weight all the rest of the way. The dinner, bacon and sliced, fried beef and soup and rice and cheese, all mixed together, came close to satisfying us.

On the next day we rested. For all the troubles we had had on the col, we were reluctant to leave it. Moreover, carrying any more food than we had to back down seemed stupid. We worried a little about the descent because we had pulled the ropes off the steep ice cliff and had no way of finding it now. But on the climb of the 11,780-foot peak, we had looked for, and apparently found, another route down that avoided the ice cliff completely.

July 16 began clear again but grew cloudy toward afternoon. We lay reading but found the books of little

interest. Don went outside to set up his bivouac tent;
later I scanned the whole mountain carefully with binoculars. In the afternoon we walked over to the edge
of the col, where there was a great prong of rock overlooking the West Fork Glacier. In a niche of rock, just
in case we should ever come back, we left the extra fixed
ropes and a bottle of cooking gas, in a plastic bag, as a
little cache. From the prong I looked for some trace
below of our snowshoes at the "dismal" camp, where
we had left them. We would need them for traversing
toward Mount Hayes. I saw something at about the
right place but couldn't be sure that it wasn't a crevasse
or a ball of snow.

We ate four meals that day, finishing with an extra
breakfast. As we had feared, it was hard to cut back
after our splurge. We had fondly imagined that the day
of double meals would give our bodies a store of food
to keep us satisfied for most of a week. By the next day,
however, we were at least as hungry as before. By now
we were sure the hunger could not be purely psychological. We had begun to find it easy to get tired; normally, by this stage of an expedition, we would have
been in superb shape and would have taken strenuous
days in stride.

The 17th began in a warm, wet storm. We put off
our departure until the next morning. Now that we
were not pushing, we began to sleep irregularly again.
Both of us dreamed often and woke often. To his relief, Don's dreams seemed to have lost their aspects of
horror; in one of them, he was back in California on a

mild summer day, with some high school friends, eating a picnic in the country. I had another banquet dream, but this time I was the host, and friend after friend kept showing up and complimenting me on the food. Both Don and I felt heavy with nostalgia, but if we tried to talk about it, we tended to antagonize each other. Strangely enough, for all the nostalgia, we had felt almost no sexual urge, and our dreams never took an overtly sexual turn. Perhaps the craving for food had subsumed our less basic sexual needs. The other pleasures that we might normally have missed seemed similarly irrelevant. For instance, I had always wished, on shorter trips, that I could hear classical music, and I had always been able to entertain myself for hours by "playing" records in my mind. On other trips I had dreamed about composing, or about spending an afternoon with Beethoven. But on Deborah, after the first few days, I missed music not at all, nor did it take any place in my dreams. My fantasies were filled with conversations, as were my dreams—endless, lyrical, warmhearted conversations (though Don, of course, was never a participant). He and I, apparently, could not talk well enough together. On the 17th we had a long argument about mannerisms, each of us trying to justify why the other's habits were unpleasant or annoying. It was our first drawn-out verbal fight in quite a while; much as we needed it, it saddened both of us.

I sensed that the wonderful cohesion of the last few days was coming to an end. In the absence of danger, hard work, and the suspense of discovery, our getting along was less vital. Whenever life was easy or dull, it was hardest—the tiny fears and resentments began to chafe us again. Nor did we have a clear goal ahead of us any more. The traverse to the other basin would be plodding work, and we felt real anxieties about finding our airdrop.

The wind sprang up overnight and blew the wet storm off. We got up at 3:00 A.M. on the 18th to pack up the camp, which we had occupied for nearly three weeks. As we started off at 5:40 A.M., we both looked back at the route, then at the col; the bare snow surprised me, and I felt a pang of regret. The sixty-pound packs were an unwelcome burden; for days we had been allowed to forget what a heavy load felt like. Still, we made it back to the crossing of the ridge in only an hour. On the south side, we traversed in the gray light of morning, roughly in the line that we had followed on the way up, then two pitches farther, rounding a corner. From there we descended a steep snow slope. At the bottom it grew icy in patches. We had to belay for six rope-lengths; with the heavy packs, it was a real nuisance. We quickly got cold belaying, and our calves and ankles began to ache from the constant effort of cramponing the slope. At last we reached the gentler glacier and for a while made fine speed downward. We were walking, most of the time, on the lumpy debris of dozens of avalanches. Because of this obvious proof of the danger of the slope in the daytime, we were anxious to get down fast. By 9:30 A.M. we had rejoined our ascent route, just at the spot where we had dangerously camped between avalanche tracks on the last day of June. From here it was a short distance to the "dismal" camp site, but all at once the going got very rough. We began plunging thigh-deep with each step. Even though we were going downhill, it became a terrible effort. At each step we had almost to roll out of the previous one, then step back up to the surface, only to have the next foot plunge all the way in again. With the heavy packs it became nearly intolerable. I stretched a crotch muscle painfully on a long step, and one of Don's ankles seemed to bother him. It took two more hours to travel the short distance to our snowshoes. We were quite happy to find them, buried except for their tips in the snow. We flopped down on our packs and ate the last bits of our lunches.

We put on our snowshoes and started back to base camp. The snow was sloppily wet, but at least we could stay on the surface, which made it easy trudging. By 1:00 P.M. we were back at base camp. We found the three food boxes and the long cache-marking pole just as we had left them. Obviously no one, man or animal, had happened by since we had left base camp almost a month before. We pitched our tent in the same spot that we had used originally and put a plastic sheet over the top in case it should snow or (for it was possible in this miserable warmth) rain. Glancing up at the col and the sharp ridge beyond, we felt removed from our weeks of combat not by hours, but by days; not by three thousand feet, but by a whole world.

For a few moments we took some interest in reread-

ing the wadded and soggy newspapers with which we
had stuffed the boxes for dropping. Political maneu-
vers, pictures of movie stars, baseball scores—they all
seemed dead and trivial. This reaction might have been
strange in view of our nostalgia for the outside world.
But we were beginning to sense vague apprehensions
about getting back, too—unanalyzable but real, for
both of us.

As Don was inside the tent cooking dinner and I was
scooping snow into the pots outside, I discovered a
handful of brown rice and little chunks of meat scat-
tered in the snow. For a moment an insane picture of
Don throwing away our precious food flashed through
my mind. Then I realized that it must have been an
extra bit of one of our first dinners, at the end of June,
which we had not been able to eat and had thrown out.
Extra food! The thought was obscene. I considered
scooping up the rice, but it looked spoiled. I called
Don's attention to it. We both stared at the food, ap-
palled by our former wastefulness, wondering how the
rations could ever have seemed so ample.

In the tent, we prepared for sleep. We felt an unfamiliar sense of freedom because our tent needed no
maintaining, no shoveling loose from the drifts, and because we could walk around safely outside. But with the
ease came the inevitable lethargy and depression. As I
crawled into my sleeping bag, something floating in the
stuffy air caught my eye. It was a mosquito, blown up
on the glacier by a stray wind perhaps. It wandered
weakly, air-starved, around the tent, then lighted on my

hand. I watched it as, oblivious to the nearness of its food or too near death to manage a bite, it stood there, motionless. Then the mosquito tried its wings, wobbled in the air, and fell to the floor of the tent. I flicked it out the door with my finger.

10 ▲

The summer was shortening; August would be upon us in another two weeks. On the col, we had noticed the gradually longer and darker nights. Now that we were low again, beneath the shadow of the mountain, and now that we had to return to a schedule of moving at night, the darkness seemed to be daily spreading and deepening. It was no longer possible to read at midnight in the tent; even at 10:00 P.M. or 2:00 A.M. it was a strain on our eyes. A few days earlier, near midnight, I had seen a twinkle of light on the tundra, far to the south. It was so faint that I had great trouble pointing it out to Don, but at last he verified it. Perhaps, we thought, it might be the hunting lodge where we had left our truck. That was the nearest dwelling we knew of. To the north, from our high camp, we had never seen the slightest sign of animate life, not even a bird or a bear. Still, we had always preferred to look north rather than south because that was where the sun set and most of the storms came from, and because it was where we had never been.

We had determined not to waste a single day on the glaciers, even during storms, because we would be doing mere load-hauling and could not afford to use up our food too quickly. But we were so tired from the muscle-straining descent that when July 19 began in a wet snowstorm, we declared a rest day. We had a few new books to read: I managed to use up the day with a Steinbeck novel, but Don could not get involved in reading.

We wanted to carry all our supplies in one load, but when we figured out the weight of everything, it dictated 85-pound packs. Reluctantly, we agreed to relay the equipment in two loads. I became aware of what seemed at the time an absurd paradox: the more we ate, the lighter our loads would be. For instance, by waiting one storm day, we had cut out three pounds of food.

The storm continued all day. We stayed dry only by virtue of the plastic sheet over the tent. By nightfall it had begun to clear, and we noticed a welcome drop in the temperature. We got off by 10:30 P.M., packing up only about thirty-five pounds of gear each. In the gloomy twilight we laced on our snowshoes, roped up, and set off. Because of an unusual cold (we recorded 24°), the snow surface of the glacier was nicely frozen —most of the way it was like walking a sidewalk. We found the going almost pleasant, though the loss of visual detail in the night made our hike hypnotically monotonous. In a little more than an hour we had covered three miles, reaching a low point at 5600 feet, where the glacier branched in four directions. We stopped at a sunken hole, the size of a tiny lake, that had filled with melt water. After a tricky approach on snowshoes, we managed to fill our water bottles and drink heartily. It was the first water we had seen since the third day of the expedition, the first since then that we had drunk without having to melt it from snow. As we sat, drinking and resting, we caught sight of two pale stars in the sky, the first we had seen on the whole trip. The glacier was wrapped in an eerie silence that seemed to urge us to get moving again.

I started off in the lead. The glacier sloped imperceptibly uphill, and we noticed that it seemed harder to keep up our fast pace. There was nothing for me to do but stare wearily ahead; nothing for Don but to keep the rope stretched between us and to avoid stepping on it. But gradually, as in the slow-motion sequence of some dreams, the scenery changed and the gray light turned brighter. We began to see the other side of Mount Hess and to catch glimpses of the precipice we had overlooked from the summit of our unnamed peak,

"11,780." Ahead of us, getting closer by achingly small stages, was a rim of snow, the pass to the Susitna Glacier. We would try only to get to the foot of it today. Two days later, perhaps, we would cross it: after that, cross another pass to the Gillam Glacier, and yet another, the steepest of all, to the basin of our airdrop. All the while we would be hiking east within the range toward Mount Hayes.

We had hoped to go all the way to the foot of the pass before eating, but our resolve faltered, and we stopped for half a lunch at a blank spot on the snow. Afterward, as we neared the pass, we discovered several huge crevasses, invisible from below, that stretched across our path. Patiently we skirted them. When we had reached an altitude of seven thousand feet, just three hundred feet below the pass, we stopped and dumped our loads. The pile of supplies looked ludicrously small; getting it there, however, had been the object of the whole day's work. We dashed back to our eating spot, where we had the rest of lunch. It was gone in no time, and we were still hungry. We talked about the food. Both of us felt that three meals a day didn't give us enough energy or incentive for a day's work. We decided to increase our intake permanently to four meals. We would follow the same rotation, but eat, for instance, a breakfast after dinner. It was a hard choice because it meant the twelve days' food that we had would last only nine. But all it had to do was get us to our airdrop—then we could eat like kings. Unless . . . the "unless" hung in our minds: unless the airdrop was buried beyond discovery. Then the nine days' food would have to get us out as well, and from that basin it could take six, or even seven days.

We got up and started back. The sun was coming up; for a while we amused ourselves with the new sights. But the monotony wore its way back into our minds, and we grew tired. We stopped for water again at the hole, then hurried on. Following Don, I stared glumly at the snow in front of my feet. Here and there I saw dark specks on the snow; they proved to be dead or weakly crawling mosquitoes. There was not a single one with much life in it. A little farther on, I saw a larger black mark on the snow, like a rock. It turned out to be a dead bird, a finch perhaps. It was cupped in a little pocket of ice as if it had hit with great impact. More likely, though, the dark lump of its body had melted the pocket into the glacier. Superstitiously, I avoided touching it.

Don was impatient to keep moving, so we started on. The last mile was the worst. I kept playing mental games to delay my boredom, but every step seemed to be sapping strength from a last reserve. At 5:30 A.M. we were back. We had covered twelve miles in seven hours, and our legs and shoulders ached from the strain. Perhaps it was the change from a routine of difficult climbing that made us so tired; still, both Don and I remembered days in California or Colorado when twelve gentle miles had been simply a pleasant hike.

Then, for all our tiredness, we slept poorly. It took

both of us hours to doze off, and we always felt only inches deep in sleep. We woke often and stayed awake from about 3:00 P.M. on. The more we tried to sleep in the afternoon, the harder it came. Worse yet, as long as we were awake, we felt hungry. At last, around 8:00 P.M., we both fell into deep sleep. I happened to awake shortly after midnight and peered drowsily at the watch. Every instinct urged me to go back to sleep, but I pulled myself together and woke Don. We didn't get off until 2:00 A.M. We felt sleepy and grouchy. The going wasn't bad at first, but we were aggravated by sore muscles and by the beginnings of heel blisters from the snowshoe bindings. With nothing else to concentrate on, the little pains grew in our minds and put us on edge. If I occasionally stepped on the rope, Don, leading, would feel a slight tug. Normally it wouldn't have bothered him, but it was an annoyance now, so that he would stop and look around, even though he knew what it was. I would wave the rope and mutter, "Sorry," which inevitably set loose a counterannoyance in me.

We had half a lunch at the water hole, spending the time in irritated silence. As we started off after lunch, I let Don lead again, since I felt too lethargic to set the pace. Reaching the low point, I glanced to the right, where the West Fork Glacier stretched south toward the lowlands. We were less than a day from the track of our hike in. It would only take four or five days to get out that way. All at once I realized that I felt more urge to hike out than to go on. Perhaps once we got to the new basin I would feel like climbing again. But there were so many uncertainties: not only the chance that the airdrop was buried, but the chance that the last pass leading to it might be too steep, on the far side, to descend safely. And what was wrong with us? We had increased our water intake, in case it was dehydration; for the same reason we had started taking salt tablets. But we seemed to be feeling worse every day. Above all, I was sick of Don. It was an effort now not to get mad all the time, not to let the irritations erupt. As I watched his sturdy form plodding ahead of me, I thought how much I would have preferred that it be someone else—someone I could talk to better or climb with more amicably.

The "escape route" to my right seemed to tug at my emotions. But I would not admit it to Don, or even to myself. We had agreed on the whole expedition, not just on Deborah. I didn't want to be the one to "crump." Besides, it was a momentary urge that had come to me while I was feeling bad. There was, after all, nothing except an accident that could force us out now. And an accident seemed impossible on such dull, level terrain. The only remote possibility was a fall into a crevasse; but we hadn't had any trouble on the whole glacier with crevasses—only up on the mountain. Besides, an accident was likely to involve both of us. Illness, perhaps—maybe we were catching some disease. But there were almost no germs up here; even the mosquitoes could not survive. It would take something like appendicitis to force us out. I imagined Don hurt, or too sick to move. The radio was worthless; it would mean I would have to hike out alone, leaving Don with food and the tent. As much as I was fed up with Don, the loneliness of a solitary hike out seemed much worse. And what if it were the other way around, with Don hiking out while I waited? That loneliness would be even more terrible.

I decided to stop dwelling on such morbid possibilities. As we began the long uphill hike, we slowed down. Soon we were nearly staggering. Even so, I found Don's pace too fast, so I asked to go first. When I led, our progress was pathetic. I would wander listlessly for a few hundred steps, then stop and crouch, arms on my knees, for breath and rest. Don was annoyed by the frequent stops, but he needed rests himself. In addition, the snow was warm again (it was 33° all night), and our snowshoes kicked up a skim of slush. When we reached the cache at seven thousand feet, it was all we could do to set up the tent and crawl inside, where we could begin cooking a precious dinner.

I expected to sleep well on account of my tiredness, but I woke after a few hours and could not get back to sleep. I still felt enervated. At 3:00 P.M. I took three quarters of a sleeping pill. It did no good; I stayed awake, uninterested in anything, with a stale taste in my mouth. At last, around eight, I fell asleep. We both awoke around 11:00 P.M. The last thing either of us wanted to do was to go outside, pack up loads, and set out again. Don had slept poorly too during the day, and he especially was in favor of sleeping some more. From a feeling of duty, however, I talked him into climbing.

While we cooked breakfast, we mentally divided the load, as we had each of the last few days, so that it would be easier to pack once we got outside. The worse we had been feeling, the more important it seemed to us to make sure we divided the weight evenly. We had a pretty good idea what a given item weighed, but each of us tried to overestimate the weight if he planned to carry the item himself and underestimate otherwise. The pound was not a fine enough unit; we haggled over ounces. The ritual took on the same absurd importance that our food division had. In the backs of our minds we knew it was silly; at the same time each of us thought the other was doing his best to cheat him. We vacillated between the roles of accuser ("Come on now, the stove's easily two and a half pounds") and martyr ("It's all right, I'll take it anyway"). For a while I labored under the obsession that Don, since he was forty pounds heavier than I, should carry more weight; I might eventually have voiced the complaint had I not suddenly realized that, by the same argument, he needed more food than I.

We got started that morning, July 22, in the dark just after midnight. The temperature seemed stuck at a treacherous 33° or 34°; the snow was in deplorable condition, and the last steep section below the pass seemed ready to avalanche. Climbing in crampons was a welcome switch, however. At the top of the pass we got the momentary pleasure of a new view. But the Susitna Glacier below was shrouded in mist, and we could see very little of it. I started down the other side. It was a steep slope, longer than the West Fork side, laced with loose rock, gravel, and, where the gravel was particularly rotten, a kind of mud. As I descended, the rope pulled loose a fairly large rock. I tried to dodge, but it rolled down and hit me in the side. Infuriated more than hurt, I yelled illogically at Don to watch what he was doing. He yelled back that he didn't know what I was talking about.

At the bottom of the slope we conferred about which direction to head next. We could see almost nothing. The map offered a few clues; Don set off for a prong of rock we could glimpse in the dim mist. I was feeling terrible. I had to take frequent rests. Don felt all right by now, but I was overcome by a feeling of lassitude. At last I told him I didn't think I could go much farther and still have the energy left to get back over the pass to our tent. He seemed irked but consented to turning around. We cached our loads and started back.

We found a less rocky route back up to the pass and stumbled over it down to camp, arriving at seven in the morning. In the six and a half hours, we had managed to move our loads the pitiful distance of one mile. After breakfast we each took a sleeping pill.

This time our insomnia vanished. Instead, we slept for twenty-two hours straight. During this phenomenal period we were in a steady, drugged, dreamless stupor. We awoke feeling much better, if still logy; but the sleep, the longest either of us had ever had in our lives, seemed but another proof that something was wrong.

We ate a breakfast, waited a short while, then ate another. Even though we had accomplished no work during the twenty-two-hour sleep, we felt, irrationally, that we had got ahead of our food schedule by going so long without eating.

We were ready to go at 12:30 P.M. Both of us moved lackadaisically as we packed up the camp. Once we got going, Don began to feel better, but I remained listless and tired. We reached the spot where we had left our previous loads by 2:30 P.M. Don had noticed that his watch seemed to stop occasionally; several times he had had to shake it to start it. We wondered if it had lost any time yet—without it, it was impossible to tell the hour, except vaguely at night. We ate a full lunch, sitting on our previous loads. It was a fairly nice day, much clearer than the misty night when we had last been there. We could easily see where the pass to the Gillam lay, about a mile to the northeast of us. I was reluctant to move; only resting and eating seemed interesting to me. I voiced some of my fears to Don about reaching the airdrop and not finding it; he listened in patient but hostile silence. The admission of my fears gave Don more assurance in the opposite direction and more determination, perhaps, to oppose me. After I had spoken, he tried calmly to answer my objections, but we could not agree. Later, he wrote in his diary, "To me Dave's fears seemed ridiculous."

We added the cache to our loads, which made our packs weigh about 75 pounds each, perhaps the most we had carried yet. Fortunately, the glacier seemed in no worse shape in the afternoon than it had in the middle of the night: the temperature still hovered around 34°. We slogged upwards toward the 7200-foot pass. Two or three times Don stuck a foot in a crevasse hole, but each time it was easy to pull the foot out and step across. I began to feel a little better and took the lead for the last stretch below the summit of the pass.

On the pass we rested. A sharp wind whipping across it dried the sweat on our bodies quickly and began to chill us. But we were thrilled; to the north, clouds reeled in and out among half a dozen handsome mountains, three of which were possible objectives for us, once we reached the airdrop. Everything around the Gillam Glacier looked bold and clean in contrast to the dirty gray of the Susitna's walls. The floor of the glacier, five hundred feet below, looked clean and smooth. Best of all, across the glacier, like troops surrounding a general, the walls of dark blue schist seemed to center on a shining cliff of whitish-brown rock: no doubt the rare, solid granite found here and there in the ranges of Alaska. What climbing we could do on good rock like that!

We changed to crampons and descended to the floor of the Gillam. As soon as we reached level snow, at 6700 feet, we stopped and pitched camp. Toward evening it began to snow lightly, so we put the plastic fly over the tent. We felt better during dinner, almost relaxed and friendly. We were less than three miles from the last pass; even though it was a very high pass

(9100 feet), we had hopes of getting to it the next day. After dinner we would be down to six days' food at four meals a day, or eight days' food at three a day. We did not want to cut back again; even four meals was far too little to keep us satisfied for twenty-four hours.

The daytime schedule seemed to agree with us much better; stalking across the flat, soundless glacier at night had always been unpleasant. Besides, we were sleeping more regularly now; that night, indeed, we slept very soundly.

11 ▲

We woke comfortably late the next morning and daw-
dled over breakfast. When we looked out, we saw that
a beautiful day had dawned on the Gillam Glacier; it
was virtually windless, and a strong sun warmed us and
dried the tent and sleeping bags. We were packed up by
12:30 P.M. As soon as we had put on our snowshoes
and hefted our packs, we looked over all the glacier,
which was blindingly white with sun. The snow looked
perfectly smooth, but here and there we could see pale,
diagonal hollows that suggested crevasses. Don led off.
Only fifty yards from camp he stuck his foot into a cre-

vasse. He yelled back to me, "Give me a belay." I put my axe in the snow and knelt, as he gingerly stepped across. Then we were both moving again.

Perhaps sixty yards farther, Don suddenly plunged into a crevasse and stuck, shoulder-deep. Immediately I thrust my axe into the snow and took in slack. Then I waited for Don to crawl out. I was not terribly worried: I had belayed a few crevasse plunges like this on McKinley, and Don had belayed me in one near the summit of our 11,780-foot peak. I even grew slightly impatient as Don seemed to thrash around helplessly.

But then he yelled, "I'm choking!" I was alarmed; I imagined the pack strap or the edge of the crevasse cutting off Don's wind.

I waited a few more seconds, but it was obvious Don couldn't get out. Perhaps rashly, I took off my pack, untied myself from the rope, tied the rope to my axe, and thrust it in again for an anchor. It didn't seem solid enough, so I quickly took our spare ice axe from my pack and tied the rope to that too. Then I walked quickly up to Don. I could not really see the crevasse at all, but I could see that Don was wedged pretty deeply in it. His hands clawed at the snow, but he said that his snowshoed feet were dangling loose. He was not actually choking, but he was in a cramped situation. The heavy pack seemed to be the obvious problem: its straps were constricting his arms and upper body. I reached out and carefully tried to pull the pack up and back. Don screamed, "Stop! It's the only thing holding me up!" His voice was full of panic. My pulling had made him slip a little farther into the crevasse so that all but his head was below the surface. Don sensed, as his feet waved in space, that the crevasse was huge. He warned me that I was too close to the edge. I backed up about five feet. For a moment I stood there, unable to do anything.

Suddeny Don plunged into the hole. The anchoring axes ripped loose and were dragged across the snow as Don fell within the crevasse. I grabbed the rope, but it was wet and whipped violently through my hands. I heard Don's yell, sharp and loud at first, trail away and fade into the frightening depth. All at once the rope stopped. About sixty feet of it had disappeared into the hole.

An excruciating silence surrounded me. With a kind of dread, I yelled Don's name. There was no answer. I yelled twice more, waiting in the silence, and then I heard a weak, thin shout: "I . . . I'm alive." The words were a great relief, but a scare as well: how badly was he hurt? I yelled, "Are you all right?" After another pause, his voice trickled back: "I think my right thumb is broken! I hit my head and it's bleeding and my right leg is hurt!"

I ran back to reanchor the rope. From my pack I got our snow shovel, dug a pit in the wet snow, tied one of the axes to the rope again, and buried the axe in the pit, stamping down the snow on top. Perhaps in a little while the snow would freeze, making the anchor solid. Through my mind flashed all kinds of thoughts, reminders of warnings before the expedition about the dangers of going with only two men, fears of never getting Don out, the thought of his blood spilling, a curse for the worthless radio.

When the snow had broken around him, Don's first impressions had been of bouncing against ice and of breaking through ice: he was not aware of screaming. He expected to feel the jerk of the rope at any moment, but it had not come. Then suddenly he had been falling fast, free; he somehow supposed that I was falling with him, and he instinctively anticipated death. Once before, in an ice-gully avalanche in New Hampshire, Don had fallen eight hundred feet—but he had been knocked out that time and had remembered only the beginning. This time he stayed conscious throughout the terrible fall.

At last there was a crushing stop, followed by piles of ice and snow falling on top of him in the darkness. Then it was still. The fear of being buried was foremost. He fought his way loose from the ice; some of the blocks were heavy, but he was able to move them and scramble out. He realized that, miraculously, he had landed on his back, wedged between two walls of ice, with the heavy pack under him to break his fall. His hands hurt, his leg felt sharply painful, and his head rang from a blow. He became aware of my shouting, the sound weak and distant, and yelled an answer upwards. As his eyes grew used to the dark, he could see where he was.

The inside of the crevasse was like a huge cavern. The only light came from the small hole, appallingly far above, and from a dim seam in the ceiling that ran in a straight line through the hole: the continuation of the thinly covered crevasse. The bottom was narrow, and the walls pressed in on him, but about thirty feet above him the space bulged to the incredible width of a large room. Above that, the walls narrowed again, arching over him like a gothic roof. Don began to glimpse huge chunks of ice, like the ones that had fallen and shattered with him on the way down, stuck to the ceiling like wasps' nests.

When I had got the anchor buried, I returned to the edge of the crevasse and shouted again to Don. With great presence of mind, he realized how possible it would be for me to fall in too, and shouted, "Dave! Be careful! Don't come near!"

His voice was so urgent that I immediately backed up to a distance of twenty feet from the little hole. But it was much harder to hear each other now. We were shouting at the tops of our lungs; had there been any wind, we could never have heard each other.

Fortunately, Don's bleeding had stopped. Struggling loose from the debris had reassured him that he wasn't seriously hurt; in fact, the thumb seemed only badly sprained instead of broken. Industriously, he got his crampons loose from his pack and put them on in place of his snowshoes. He still had his axe; chopping steps and wedging upward between the walls, he got to a place where he could see better. At once, he discovered the real nature of the subsurface glacier: corridors and chambers, at all depths, shot off in every direction. The whole thing was hideously hollow. At first Don had thought he might climb out; now he realized it would be impossible. But he had a furious desire to get out. He had put on his mittens but was getting cold anyway. Around him, on all sides, water was dripping and trickling: it was impossible to stay dry.

Don became obsessed with warning me away from the edge. If I fell in too, there would be no chance for either of us to get out. I stood still, outside; I could see only the small hole and had little idea in which direction the crevasse ran. Don, on the other hand, could tell which way it ran but had no idea where I was. With a confused series of shouts we managed to orient with respect to each other.

We both realized Don's pack had to come out first. We could not afford to leave it there. He could not wear it on the way out; I would have to haul it up. It would not be safe at all for Don to untie from the rope; I might never be able to feed the end back down to him. But it was the only rope we had. I racked my brain for an alternative. There was some nylon cord in the repair kit, which was in my pack. I ran back and got it out—it was not nearly long enough. Then I remembered our slings and stirrups, nylon loops and ladders we had brought for the technical climbing on Deborah. I dug them out, untied all the knots, found some spare boot laces, and finally tied everything together in one long strand. When it was done, I threw the end into the hole and lowered it. Don yelled that it reached.

He had taken his pack apart. Now he tied his sleeping bag onto the end of the line, and I pulled it up. But as the load neared the top, the line cut into the bad snow at the edge of the crevasse. Just below the top, the load caught under the edge. I jerked and flipped the line, to no avail. Don saw the problem but could think of no solution.

It became obvious that I had somehow to knock loose the rotten snow from the edge. But I didn't dare get near the hole, and Don would be standing beneath all the debris I might knock down. I could imagine only one way to do it.

I checked the rope's buried anchor again: it seemed solidly frozen in. I pulled and jerked on the rope, but it wouldn't budge. With one of the nylon slings I had left, I tied a loop around my waist, then tied a sliding knot to the main rope with it. When I pulled, the knot would hold tight; but when I let up, the knot would slide. Don, meanwhile, had found a relatively shielded place to hide. I inched toward the hole, carrying an axe and the shovel. If the edge broke, I should fall in only a few feet: then I might be able to scramble back out. I got no closer than I had to, but finally I was within two feet of the dangerous edge. The rope was stretched tight behind me. I squatted and reached out with my axe. The stuff broke loose easily and plunged noisily into the crevasse. As the hole enlarged, I slipped the knot tighter and waddled back a foot or so. Some of the snow had to be dug loose; some fell at the blow of the axe. It was awkward work but it was profitable. At last I had dug back to bare, hard ice. The rope would not cut into it. Leaning over, I peered into the awesome cavern. At first I could see only darkness; moments later, I glimpsed the faint outline of Don below, much more distant than I had even imagined.

I retreated from the hole and resumed hauling Don's sleeping bag; this time it came easily. One by one, I fished out the pieces of Don's load. With each, we grew more optimistic. The pack frame itself was hardest— its sharp corners caught on the ice; but at last I shook it loose and jerked it out.

Now there was only Don himself to get out. There was no possibility of hauling him. He would have to use the sliding knots on stirrups, which would support his feet, to climb the rope itself. I dangled some stirrups into the hole for him. He yelled when he got them. Then I retreated to the anchor, added my weight to the solidity of the frozen snow, and waited.

Slowly, painfully, Don ascended the rope. Everything was wet, so he had to tie an extra, tighter loop in the knots. This made them tend to jam, and he had to claw them loose several times. He was shivering now, soaking wet, and tired; in addition, his sprained fingers made handling the knots clumsy and painful. But from time to time he shouted his progress, and each time his voice sounded stronger and closer.

The weather was still perfect, but the sun had traveled far into the western part of the sky A full four hours had elapsed since Don had fallen in. The peaks, as intriguing as ever, towered out of the smooth, apparently harmless surface of the glacier.

At last Don's head poked out of the hole. I cheered him on, but I was struck by the shaky tiredness I could see in his face. He crawled out of the hole and sat gasping on the edge. I came up to him, full of a strong impulse of loyalty, and put my arm around his shoulders, telling him he had done a good job. We ate a few bites of lunch—the minute the emergency was over, it seemed, our appetites returned.

We decided simply to backtrack the hundred yards to the camp site and pitch the tent again. I gathered the pieces of Don's pack and loaded it up. We staggered back to the fresh platform, very careful as we recrossed the first crevasse. In the subtle light of afternoon, looking back eastward toward the mountains we had been trying to reach, we could see faint blue line after faint blue line intersecting our potential path, parallel marks indicating a dozen farther crevasses like the one Don had fallen into.

I repitched the tent while Don rested. Inside, we looked at his injuries. He was badly bruised, especially on the right thigh; his head was bruised, with a small cut showing through blood-matted hair; half his fingers were sprained, the thumb badly. But it was a blessing there was no injury worse than that. Gradually, Don warmed up as his clothes dried out. We cooked dinner and ate, with a sense of peace and reprieve. Afterward, as it grew dark, we each took a sleeping pill; within a few minutes we were deep in slumber.

12 ▲

In the morning, when we awoke, we found the watch had stopped. We set it arbitrarily and started breakfast. Don was stiff and sore from his injuries, but the sleep had done him good. In my mind there was no question now but that we had to hike out to civilization. I was pretty sure Don would agree; even so, I was reluctant to bring up the matter. Finally I did. To my surprise, Don was set on going on.

We argued for more than an hour. I listed all the reasons for my decision. First, we were down to five days' food (perhaps seven, if we stretched it), and the hike out, we thought, would take about five days. If we went two days farther toward the airdrop basin, we might be forced into a seven-day hike out on only three days' food. And we had encountered only one of the obviously many hideous crevasses on this glacier. I argued that we had been very lucky to get Don out alive and that nothing would keep us from falling into another crevasse. The snow conditions, as we had found, were no better at night. Moreover, part of the hike-out route, to the south down the Susitna Glacier and River, was off our maps, since we hadn't anticipated it: who could say what obstacles we might run into? The radio was worthless, we were constantly hungry, and Don was bruised all over.

Despite all this, Don was determined to push on. He did not want it to be his accident and his injuries that stopped us. We could hike up the glacier on its southern edge, he argued, where the crevasses would be small enough to be safe. He was as eager as ever to climb the peaks ahead, and he was willing to go without food a few days, if need be, so long as we could definitely ascertain whether or not our airdrop was buried.

Don's stand put me in a strange situation. I was torn between admiration for and fear of him: at once he seemed terribly brave and terribly foolish. I remembered his insistence, early on the expedition, on going ahead the night he had been feeling dizzy and losing his balance. I wondered now if he wasn't expressing the same kind of overreaction: if so, it seemed a kind of madness. My inner voice, with its calculation of risks and complications, seemed to be speaking pure common sense, while Don's was fanatic. At the same time I could not help wondering if I was quitting on him, panicking prematurely. After all, before the accident I had been the one who was anxious for the trip to be over. I remembered the urge toward the safe south I had felt that dreary night, a week before, hauling loads across the West Fork Glacier. Perhaps I was "crumping"; perhaps I was not good enough for Don.

Our argument was uncommonly restrained, and for once we seemed objective and frank, as if a residue of respect for each other had settled out of the recent accident. I admitted that I was afraid of the glacier; Don granted that he didn't look forward to getting back to California. But I was possessed with a feeling that Don had gone slightly crazy, or that the crevasse fall had done something to him. I even fancied that the blow on his head had distorted his reason. At one point, as we were arguing about food, he said, "I'd almost rather starve here than go out now." Each symptom of fanaticism, like this one, made me look at Don in a more curious light. Yet I could not bear to attack his motives, as I had before, so soon after his ordeal in the crevasse. Don interpreted my reluctance to force the decision as a cowardice about taking the responsibility for it, which it may partly have been; all the same, I wanted the decision to be both of ours, so that we could not recriminate later.

Gradually, with heavy heart, Don saw that I was firmly set on hiking out. He could not be as staunchly in favor of going ahead—he naturally recoiled at the thought of falling into another crevasse. At last he gave in and agreed with me. I tried not to gloat over the relief I felt, and Don concealed his bitterness. We got dressed and packed up the camp in a marvelous spirit of reconciliation, a spell of grace over our life of antagonism. When we were ready to leave, we called it 2:00 P.M. With wistful glances back at the mountains we would never reach, still holding out their clean arms to us under a warm sun, we started trudging back up the pass to the Susitna Glacier.

My spirits, as always when the doubts and fears that had gnawed inside me were resolved, rose to exuberance. At first Don could not share my feeling, but his disappointment softened. On the climb to the pass we made up four or five verses, to the tune of "The Cowboy's Lament" ("As I walked out in the streets of Laredo"), about the crevasse accident. Instead of funeral roses, we pictured sacrificial piles of our favorite foods all over the glacier. One verse seemed particularly poignant:

It was once with my ice axe I used to go dashing,
Once in my crampons I used to go gay,
First over to Deborah, then down to the Gillam,
But I've broken my thumb, and I'm dying today.

At the top of the pass, we stopped to rest and gathered our last look to the north. Our marks on the snow eloquently told our story. Below us was a flat rectangular patch, where the tent had been pitched. From it a short track led straight east until it abruptly ended in a little hole. There were stray marks around the hole, but the snow lay untouched beyond.

We turned and headed down the Susitna Glacier. For a mile I led, here and there picking out our tracks from two days before, where they still showed under an inch of new snow. At the corner, the tracks turned west toward the pass we had crossed from the West Fork Glacier. We continued straight down the Susitna. We had only about a thousand feet of altitude still to drop before we would reach the nevé line, below which all the snow had melted, leaving bare ice, with the crevasses exposed and safe. But there were still quite a few crevasses to cross. I led for another half mile, through what seemed to be the worst of it. I was nervous about the hidden cracks and stuck my foot through a couple of snow bridges. However, the crevasses didn't look as big as the ones on the Gillam. Still, Don belayed me over any stretch that looked dubious, and we carefully skirted the obvious crevasses. It was slow going. As we seemed to enter a comparatively safe plateau, Don took the lead. The snow was soft and wet, scalloped with confusing sun cups. At about 4:00 P.M. he stopped to ponder an apparent pair of crevasses that nearly touched end to end. At the other end of the rope, I kept the line almost taut between us. Don started to cross what he thought was a little island of snow between the crevasses. Suddenly the island collapsed. I saw Don disappear and plunged the axe in immediately, crouching for the shock. A little pull came but it didn't budge me. I supposed Don had fallen about five feet and waited for him to scramble out. But there was no sign of him. Without getting up, I yelled, "Are you all right?" After a moment I heard his weak, distant voice, tinged with something like hysteria: "I've stopped bleeding, I think!"

With a gust of weariness and fear, I thought, "Not again!" I shouted, "How far in are you?"

Don's voice came back, "Thirty feet . . . there's blood all over in here. I've got to get out of here quick!" He sounded beaten, as if a vital string in him had broken.

When the island had collapsed, he had fallen slightly backward into the crevasse. The nylon rope had stretched and cut back into the near bank, allowing Don to fall as far as thirty feet. But this time the walls were only three or four feet apart. He had smashed his face brutally on a shelf of ice halfway down.

Outside, I imagined having to go through all the emergency procedure of evacuation again and hurriedly got out our hauling line. But Don, seeing that he could climb out by himself, took off his pack and snowshoes and put on his crampons. This was difficult, wedged as he was between the close walls. The crevasse, at a lower altitude than the one on the Gillam, was dripping and running with water. With the energy of panic, Don forced his way up and out of the crevasse, chimneying between the icy walls. As soon as I realized what he was doing, I pulled the rope in to try to aid him. Within a few minutes he had reached the surface.

156 ▲

I hurried over to help him. He looked scared and exhausted, on the verge of tears. His lower face was covered with blood; I winced at the sight of it. He was in an agony of pain. I made him sit down and got some codeine from the medical kit, which he managed to swallow. We got the bleeding mostly stopped. It was fairly warm, but Don was shivering uncontrollably in his soaked clothes. I helped him take off his shirt and put my own jacket on him. Don apologized for getting blood on it; I told him not to be silly, but I felt suddenly defenseless before his pathetic concern.

I changed to crampons; as Don gave me a nominal belay with one hand, I slithered down into the crevasse to get his pack. The ice on which Don had cut his face was actually sharp to the touch. The wetness was oppressive, and as I got farther into the crevasse, the darkness added to a sense of claustrophobia. I found Don's pack at a place where the walls were not much wider than my body, and tied the rope to it. Don's blood was visible on both walls of the crevasse; I felt an irrational fear of getting it on me. There was a rank smell of stale air and blood in the gloomy, wet cavern. I felt the same panicky urge to get out that Don must have felt. Quickly I chimneyed back to the top of the crevasse; then I sat, wedged feet and back, between the walls of ice, and tried to pull the pack up in one piece. It took an extreme effort, but at last I got the thing up and shoved it over the edge onto the snow. Then I crawled out of the hole myself.

Don was obviously in some kind of shock. The bleeding had essentially stopped, but his chin was a raw, ragged mess, and he could hardly talk. Despite the down jacket, he was shivering miserably. We decided to set up camp on the spot. I pitched the tent and got the stove and food out of our packs. Still, it was 7:30 P.M. before we were settled inside. The codeine had helped numb the pain, but Don was still in great suffering. He had sprained all the fingers on his left hand, so that he could barely use them. The knuckles were scraped raw. At last he could get into his sleeping bag and begin to warm up. I started the stove, which helped warm the tent, and melted snow for hot water with which to bathe Don's cuts. I daubed at the lacerations on his face with some wet cotton, but it only made the blood flow again. With pained words, Don complained of cuts inside his mouth too. I tried to look, and saw gouges on the inside of his lower cheek. Blood was getting all over the tent.

Just when we seemed to be getting the cuts clean, Don closed his mouth, and we heard a soft hissing sound as he breathed. "What's that?" he asked. With alarm, I saw bubbles of air in the blood on his chin. Checking his mouth, I found that the cut went all the way through the cheek below the lip. We both felt nauseated, but I tried to cheer him up by telling him that such things happened all the time. Finally Don settled into his bag, where he could hold a piece of cotton to his mouth to clot the blood. I cooked dinner. When it was ready, Don tried to eat, at my insistence. He found that by cutting the food into small pieces he could feed them into his mouth, chew them delicately, and swallow. This was crucial, even if it took him an hour and a half to finish a meal.

He took another pill for the pain. He seemed numb and sluggish, but he was taking the injury bravely. We divided a sleeping pill between us, Don taking three quarters and I a quarter. We would have taken more, but we felt we had to get up in the early morning, just on the chance that it might be colder and safer then. Ideally, we would have rested there the next day. But we did not have enough food and would have to push on. We had only made about two miles that day, much less than we had planned. We were down to four days' food, and we still had a mile of this treacherous glacier to cross and forty-five miles of wilderness beyond.

As I lay awake in the gathering dark, I heard Don's breathing grow deep and even. It was a blessing that he was able to sleep. Since the moment he had apologized for getting blood on my jacket, I had felt an inarticulate impulse of love for him. He had been so courageous; already he was showing signs of taking this accident, too, in stride. But I could not sleep. I imagined the morning's trek through the last of the crevasses. They were fiendish; there was no way to find them or tell how big they were: the axe could not probe far enough. And there was no way to belay across them safely. Even now, as we camped between a pair of them, I sensed the others crowding around our tent, like wolves in the night, waiting for us.

13 ▲

I awoke with the gray light of morning, at what our unreliable watch said was 4:00 A.M. The day was July 26, our thirty-eighth in a row on glaciers or mountain walls. It was already getting late; I was impatient to be off. The weather was still clear. Miraculously, it seemed substantially colder outside than it had the afternoon before. We cooked breakfast and ate it as quickly as Don's cuts would allow. Again, the rest had done him good. In the early light, inside the tent, it was hard to examine the cuts, but they seemed to have started scabbing. Don said the pain was less intense than before; in fact, he refused to take even an aspirin. We had debated whether or not to give him penicillin. Don's natural aversion to medicine made him reluctant; we thought the glacier should be pretty much germ-free and agreed that the chance of a reaction to the drugs was enough reason not to take them as long as he did not feel ill.

Don's powers of recuperation amazed me. As we packed up camp, he insisted on helping, although his swollen and blood-caked fingers made even the easiest of chores, like tying his boot laces, very difficult. As soon as I had my snowshoes on, I could tell that the snow was in much better shape; however, it had not actually frozen. I set off in the lead, full of apprehension. Don followed, ready to belay me on an instant's notice. I wove my way through a series of real crevasses and hundreds of imagined ones. We could see the bare, icy glacier in the sun half a mile below us; for all my caution, I was consumed with eagerness to get to it.

At last the snow began to thin, and at 7:30 A.M. we reached the bare ice. I stopped and pulled in rope to bring Don up to me. Our sense of relief was tangible. We took off our snowshoes for the last time, thoroughly glad to be done with the treacherous upper reaches of the glaciers. Fittingly, we had just emerged into the warm early morning sun. During a brief rest, I looked at Don's cuts. The pus had filled the hole in his lower cheek so that he could no longer breathe through it. His skin was a gruesome pastiche of black and red scab, gray pus, and white cotton; but it looked better than the open wound of the day before, and Don felt little troubled by it so long as we kept moving. He still, however, had to speak slowly and laboriously, like a man with a speech defect.

There were small channels of water gushing over the hard ice all around us; we could drink our fill at any moment. Don had trouble drinking from a water bottle but managed to get about half what he poured out into his mouth. Our overboots, which we had worn almost steadily for the last five weeks, were soaked and tattered; we took them off now and spontaneously agreed to throw them away. The act gave us a moment of almost wild enthusiasm, not only because it lightened our packs by twenty pounds, but because it stood for all the restraints and fears we could throw off, now that we were in safe, low country.

Yet there were still obstacles to worry about: rivers, especially, but also the lower part of the glacier and the eventual swamp; perhaps even wild animals. All the same, we set off again with a kind of abandon. To avoid carrying the rope, we stayed tied together; but instead of being ready to belay, we let the rope drag across the ice between us. Don took the lead and set a terrific pace down the glacier. I was amazed; it was as fast as I could go, and I had not bruised a leg recently or hit my head or lost any blood. All around us were signs of warmth and wetness and life; it was as if we were walking into a land of spring after a hard and oblivious winter. The glacial brooks and trickles made soft, rich, rushing sounds, and an easy breeze carried a breath of willow bark with it. On a rocky slope beside the glacier grew patches of green grass, impossibly green: the sight was sweet enough to taste. The sun lit the hard glacier before us like fields of crystal.

At Don's fast pace, it took us only about an hour to cover the three miles down to the junction of our glacial branch with the main fork of the Susitna Glacier. We stopped for lunch on the first big moraine, a long ridge of boulders and gravel stretching like a highway down the glacier. We climbed to its highest point for our half-lunch. Behind us to the east we could see Mount Hayes again, now nine thousand feet above us. The whole upper part of the glacier was a jungle of crevasses and shattered icefalls. We picked out the branch that led to our airdrop basin: it looked at least as broken up as the rest. A single, slender peak thrust up before Mount Hayes, a peak we had known only as "10,910"; it was the one we had most cherished the chance to climb, by all odds the sharpest and most graceful, the only one that shared something of Deborah's perfection. Now it lay tantalizingly near, only seven miles from us; but it might as well have been a hundred.

Turning to look southwest down the glacier, we could see that the middle strip of ice seemed to reach the farthest. It would be our aim only to get off the glacier today: we would hope to cross the lowlands in three more days. The sun was just warm enough to ward off the chill in the air; but even as we anticipated the warmth of the lower country, we began to long again for the high, cold, and dangerous world behind us.

Don managed to cut his sausage and candy bars into

small pieces that he could chew. But he had no way of licking the candy-bar wrappers, a procedure we had come to practice with all the pleasure of dessert, since a thin smear of chocolate had melted onto them. He gave me his wrappers instead. I felt prodigally greedy to have his to lick as well as my own; but they would have gone to waste otherwise.

The easy travel on the glacier became monotonous. For several hours we stayed roped, but when we entered a region of little ice horns on which the rope often snagged, we unroped and coiled it up. For a while after that we walked side by side, a luxury we had never enjoyed on the mountain or the upper glaciers. We chatted happily as the high walls of the surrounding peaks slowly inched by. In the distance we could see the hazy blue of the tundra, but it was scarcely distinguishable from the pale sky.

At one point I noticed a sparkling object ahead of us that somehow looked different from the ice. I kept my eye on it as we neared. When we got to it, I picked it up; to my complete surprise, it was a strip of aluminum foil, about two inches long. I showed it to Don. We felt, instead of excitement, a surge of disappointment: we had thought we were the first ever to walk on this glacier. In fact, as we realized, the little strip was the first human object not our own that we had discovered on the whole expedition. Don suggested, after some thought, that it might have been dropped by an airplane, perhaps for radar purposes in a storm. His explanation made us feel better; perhaps we were the first, after all. Farther down the glacier, we found two or three more pieces of foil. We could think of no reason for a glacier traveler to leave them, so we accepted the airplane theory. The nostalgia a human object might have aroused in us was lacking; the foil even suggested a hostile, mechanized world to which there was no reason to return. But if we thought of food, the civilized world regained its appeal.

As we got lower on the glacier, the rock debris became more prevalent, and the little rivulets began to gather into solid streams. We crossed the smaller ones easily, but as we edged toward the south side of the glacier, in hopes of leaving it, we confronted a huge torrent, thick with spray, spewing furiously downwards. Wading it was out of the question because of its speed and icy bottom, but we could find no place narrow enough to jump across. I wanted to hike back up the glacier, in hopes the stream would get smaller. Don thought it was likely the stream would drop into a hole in the glacier farther down, so he wanted to go on. We were getting tired from the loads, and our argument began to provoke old irritations. At last Don offered to scout ahead, without a pack, while I waited. I accepted rather selfishly and enjoyed the rest while Don went ahead. Soon he was back, claiming he had seen a little cloud of spray where he thought the stream might dive into the glacier. I was dubious but agreed that it was worth going ahead to investigate it. We went on, feeling slightly hostile toward each other; but I actually hoped that Don was right.

When we reached the cloud of spray, we saw that it was exactly what Don had suspected. I congratulated him, without any rancor. We stood for a moment, trying to look inside the frightening hole into which the violent water plunged. Much as we enjoyed the sight and taste and novelty of water, it seemed the last sign, and the most treacherous, of the chaotic power of the mountains we were leaving. The next few days, when we should cross the drab and otherwise peaceful tundra, the turgid rivers, born in the frozen heights we had left, would be our last reminders of that world.

A few hundred yards beyond, we crossed the empty channel in the ice where the glacial river had once run. It was deeper than we were tall. In the bottom of it, I could not escape an uneasy feeling, as if at any moment a flood of water might sweep down upon us.

From there it was a short walk to the edge of the glacier. We saw a few withered purple flowers on the edge: they seemed fragrant and beautiful. Rounding a rocky corner of the last mountain shelf, we met a carpet of rich tundra grass sprinkled with willows. The thronging greenness swept like a fire across the valley before us. We waded two tiny streams, taking off our boots. On the far side of the first, we let our toes revel in the soft tufts of grass. Simply to stand there barefoot was an intense pleasure.

Beside the second stream we set up camp. We were on the edge of our map, at 3600 feet. The grass was dry, the stream as clear as the sky. We lounged sensuously in the spongy grass: we had forgotten what a joy easy camping could be. We bathed Don's wounds again but left the core of pus in the cuts. As we prepared our chicken stew for cooking, we forgot where we were for a moment and put a pot of stream water on the stove in order to melt it to water in which to soak the stew. Everything seemed so easy: the memory of stinging blizzards in a cramped tent, when it had been a considerable effort to open the door and scoop a potful of snow, seemed as remote now as an adventure in some book.

There were a few mosquitoes around camp, but we almost welcomed them. After dinner we were, as usual, still hungry, but the feeling could not intrude on our sense of ease and luxury. We gathered willow branches for a fire and soon were sitting around the sparkling flames, gazing hypnotically into them, as we had on the first evening of the expedition. The sun set in the northwest. Deborah was silhouetted in ghostly blue against the bright sky, beyond two glaciers, as sharp as in our best dreams.

The night looked so clear that we dispensed with the tent, pitching only the plastic fly between our packs. We lay talking, half in our sleeping bags, conscious of the unfamiliar softness, like infinite mattress, under our backs. We were tired; Don fell asleep in the middle of our conversation. I lay awake for a few minutes longer, but the gentle sound of the stream soon lulled me into a deep, peaceful sleep.

In the morning we got off by 9:30 A.M. The weather was still clear and pleasantly warm. At once we were off the map. I suggested following the glacier along a side-hill, but Don vaguely remembered a short cut he had seen on the more extensive maps in Cambridge, months before, a low pass to the south that seemed to cut through the foothills. I was unsure, but Don talked me into his decision again, and for the second time he was right, saving us at least several hours' work. We found easy going over dry, soft tundra, skirting a few lakes, up to the pass. Near the highest lake we saw a solitary caribou that panicked at the sight of us and ran far up the opposite hillside.

The greenness still seemed marvelous to us, and we could not take in enough of the scenery. The country was so different from the world of glaciers: in its peculiar way, it seemed freer and emptier, even lonelier. For several hours our enthusiasm stayed high. After crossing a little stream at the top of the pass, we stopped for lunch. Again Don offered me his candy wrappers. I noticed another virtue of the gift: it took him so long to eat, with his careful chewing, that I would surely have grown impatient had I not had something else to do, like lick all the wrappers. The pain of his cuts was minimal when we were moving, Don said; it only bothered him now, really, in the evenings; hence he would take Empirin tablets only before going to sleep.

We continued across the long plateau. Below us, we knew, even though it was partly off the map, we would face the East Fork of the Susitna River, a fairly large, and probably fast, glacial stream. We were worried about crossing it; it seemed the last obstacle of all.

At 2:00 P.M. we reached the edge of the plateau. As we walked to the edge, we caught our first sight of the river. It was still more than two miles distant, and this deceived us, for it looked like a thin, harmless ribbon of blue. Confidently, we started down the long slope.

At once the mosquitoes discovered us. We walked through thick, sporadic clouds of them, batting them off with our hands and even with our ice axes. We grew suddenly tired, and the annoyance of the mosquitoes added to our weariness. The going seemed interminable. Soon we were enmeshed in thickets of willows; through the denser parts of them, we beat our way clumsily, like bears. Finally, the tundra, which had been so wonderfully springy and dry, grew soggy and sloppy with mud.

As we neared it, the river began to look bigger and bigger. What was more, it was obviously swift. All at once we were not so sure. A little after three, we stopped at a lake just overlooking the river. We sat on our packs, since we could not find dry ground. The mosquitoes attacked us in hordes, biting even through clothing and the repellent we had carefully carried all through the expedition. We could not get clear water to drink; the lake water tasted slightly rancid, but we drank it anyway. We were very tired and covered with sweat; the rest of our lunch passed in depressed silence. Our ears were alert to a nearby, ominous sound: the heavy thunder of the river that lay blocking our path.

14 ▲

The mosquitoes drove us on. We wandered downward through the dense, scratchy thickets and the soggy swamp toward the unavoidable river, looking for moose trails through the worst of the brush. Evening was approaching; we could see the huge main stream of the Susitna River, wandering across the tundra in the hazy distance. We would have liked to stop and camp, but it would not be safe until we had crossed the river.

When we reached the bank, we stood staring unhappily at the churning water. Don shouted over the stream's roar, "Looks like a rocky bottom!" We knew this would mean treacherous wading. There was no question of going barefoot here; we would have to keep our boots on to have a chance of staying on our feet in the numbing torrent. We scrambled down to the edge and took our packs off on the weed-choked bank. Then we removed our pants; at least we could try to keep them dry.

The going looked so bad that we decided to rope up. Since Don was heavier, he stayed on the bank to belay while I carefully waded in. The mosquitoes swarmed to his bare legs and he could not swat fast enough to keep them off. The water hit me with a sudden, chilling shock. I stumbled but caught my balance. At once the stream got deeper, and the farther under my legs went, the greater was the surface the water had to attack. Moving one foot at a time was a tricky business, for the current seized them at every movement, and the round rocks on the bottom were slimy and irregular. I unhooked the waist loop of my pack so that I could get rid of it in an emergency. Keeping my eyes away from the dizzying water, I tried to concentrate on the opposite bank. But by the time I got only ten feet from shore, the current was surging around my thighs. I felt just barely in balance. I looked back at Don, who seemed to be holding his breath; our glances agreed, and I returned to the bank.

We coiled the soaked rope, put on our pants again, and headed downstream. It was not easy to follow the bank, for it was steep, thick with brush and weeds, and often cut by little ravines. We fought our way about half a mile downstream, then tried again.

This time the mosquitoes were even worse. The clusters of them on our legs, the unpreventable bites, several each second, put us in a kind of panic. The water was the only place to avoid them. This time the stream looked wider, and consequently shallower. We left the rope in my pack and edged into the current, facing upstream, our arms locked together. Don went first, counting on his greater stability. At first this seemed to work. We got about forty feet out and were entering the main channel. But again we seemed only precariously in balance, and it was hard to move together. We stopped for a moment. Both of us sensed that if we lost our footing we would never regain it. The water was so cold that we could not feel our feet, and our legs ached. I shouted, "It's no good! Let's go back!"

Very carefully, we made our way back to shore. We were getting extremely tired and hated the thought of going on downstream. But it was the only choice.

A little farther on, we made our third try. It was less successful than our second. Above all, the rocks on the bottom made us nervous: they were impossible to see and treacherous to feel.

As we sat on the bank, pulling on our pants again, I felt almost like crying. I swore at the mosquitoes, blaming them for our troubles. There was one remote, dependable solution: that was to hike up the stream, perhaps as far as whatever glacier it sprang from, and cross it where it was small enough. But that could take days and an agony of effort.

I had another hunch. The main branch of the Susitna, in the flat land below us, looked slower, broader, and, most important, muddier. Perhaps, if we kept on downstream, we would get out of the rocky-bottomed region and find smoother silt under the water. It was worth a try. We continued down the bank for another half mile. I had to keep telling myself to push a little farther, to keep going, and to resist the impulse to cut down to the river too soon.

At last the river seemed to slow and broaden; it even looked muddy. But it also looked very deep. We went down to the bank, picking a part of the river where a small grassy island cut it into two channels. I started into the current first. The floor, happily, was smooth silt, and it was much easier to slide through the slower water. But it rose above my knees, above my thighs, at last to my waist, and I had to go back. Don was trying upstream from me. I watched him go in to his waist, hesitate, then forge on. All at once the water dropped to his knees again, and he easily reached the island. Jubilantly, I followed him. It went a little deeper on me, but Don coached me to the shore. The second channel was trivial by comparison. Suddenly we had crossed the river; we threw our packs down gratefully on the sand of the far shore. We hurried our pants on, trapping mosquitoes inside them. Then we decided to eat a breakfast on the spot. After all, the sun was just setting, and we had been going since nine-thirty in the morning.

The river water was thick with silt. We had to let it settle before we could drink it. For that reason we decided to go on, only as far as the first usable water, rather than camp at the river bed. As the sun's rays left us, we quickly got chilled. We were soaked above our waists, and our boots were as soggy as they could get. Tired as we felt, we were anxious to get moving again so that we could warm up. We shouldered our packs and started uphill.

Now, paradoxically, we could not find water. We had hoped to go only a few hundred yards, but we found ourselves crossing half, three-quarters, then a whole mile, desperately looking for a stream. We gave up the search for running water and agreed to settle for a pool; even if it were rancid, we could boil it. But we could not find even a puddle. The logs and bushes were covered with a dusty, deathlike moss. The mosquitoes reached a peak density, the worst we had ever seen in our lives. As we talked, we could not keep them out of our ears, noses, and mouths; some of them even flew into our eyes. The darkness was growing fast, and the swarms of mosquitoes seemed to darken the sky even more. They surrounded us with a dull, droning sound that we kept mistaking for the sound of a stream. I found myself wondering whether it was the same group of mosquitoes following us, or a constantly changing segment of a universal horde through which we passed. Don had a nylon headnet, which he put on now: it was a good thing, for the insects were driven mad by the smell of blood and pus in his cuts. I had thrown away my headnet up on the glacier in a moment of weight-saving zeal. Now I relied on repellent, but the mosquitoes ignored it, and my sweat washed it off quickly anyway.

It was growing very dark. We were on the edge of

total exasperation and exhaustion. We had to have water; the more we searched for it, the thirstier we grew. At last I caught sight of a faint glimmer from something white in a ravine to our right. We hiked down to examine it and found not water, but a small patch of caked, dirty ice that had somehow stayed frozen in this dark hollow. It was good enough for us.

With the last of our energy we gathered logs and branches for a fire, the only remedy we could think of for the mosquitoes. But when we tried to light it, the wood only smoked and smothered the flames. It was all rotten and damp inside; it was as if the greedy wood had soaked into its foul core all the water we so desperately needed.

We contented ourselves with our stove. The ice was very hard and took a long while to melt. We could not filter all the dirt out of it either. In his tiredness, Don cooked the powdered eggs wrong, and they tasted like rubber; still, we eagerly ate every scrap. We could not keep the mosquitoes out of the food or out of our mouths as we ate.

Miserably, we went to bed, too tired to pitch the tent. We crawled into our sleeping bags and pulled the rain fly over us. Don kept his headnet on; once he had grown used to the whine in his ears, he could sleep. I pulled my bag all around me, except for a tiny breathing hole. But the mosquitoes found that out and landed constantly on my nose and upper lip. I was too tired to brush them off: most of the time I tried to blow them away. But the sluggish insects ignored my puffs and bit until I squashed them.

I slept only fitfully. It rained a little in the night, but we did not get very wet. On the other hand, neither did the rain discourage the mosquitoes.

In the morning, as we got up, I felt irritable and unrested. My upper lip was a swollen mass of bites, partly blocking my nose. Don felt only a little better. We ate breakfast hurriedly and set our watch at 8:30 A.M. as we started off.

We had a fairly good idea of where we were and a vague confidence that it should take two more days to get out, barring any obstacle. We had two days' food left. Don set a good pace, contouring across the side of the long hill we had been traversing since the river. I followed him for a while in silence, but I felt tired enough so that his pace began to wear on me. At last, in an irritated voice, I asked him to slow down.

The first two or three miles were the worst. Both of us were still weak from the strenuous effort of the day before; our pace seemed to get slower and slower, our rest stops more frequent and longer. We could see, from the part of the map we carried, that we would soon have to cross another stream, a fairly big one, but by no means the size of the East Fork. With that as a goal for lunch, we tried to forget our hunger and weariness. The mosquitoes, still thick, were not as bad as the night before. The sky looked as if it might rain, and for once we hoped for it, to drive the rest of the insects away.

The going became worse. The willow and alder thickets blocked our way more often; although we followed moose trails through some of them, in others we had to crawl, like natives in a jungle. Don was carrying some long stakes and the extra ice axe on the top of his pack; they kept catching on branches and holding him back. He complained loudly about it but was too proud to ask me to carry them; I was too stubborn to offer.

The slope was so soft and so constantly tilted in the same direction that our feet began to wear blisters on the downhill sides and our ankles grew sore from correcting the tilt. We could never see very far ahead; there was always a green patch of willows before us, blocking the view. Our rests became blessed, silent intervals: each time we stopped, we would throw off our packs, collapse on the soft, matted slope, and lie gazing lethargically at the storm clouds dancing above the flat plain to the west. Somewhere out there lay the ground we had crossed forty-one days before, full of hope and energy, on the hike in.

We reached the small canyon of the expected stream before noon. From the edge we could see white froth below as the river spilled down its rocky channel. It was swift and noisy but looked small. We plunged down the bank, which was a tropical tangle of weeds and bushes, and fought our way to the edge. We happened to hit the stream where it was broken into three currents by little islands. Soon we were wading in. The knee-deep water had surprising force, but we waded across without incident. The pounding of the stream on our legs and the spray in our faces was almost exhilarating; in the middle of crossing, we bent down to drink. On the far side we scrambled out of the ravine and stopped for a first lunch.

My feelings of irritation had gradually worn off, but we were too tired to feel very friendly. Nevertheless, I reflected that we had got along better the last four days than any before, at least since the hike in. Perhaps at last we were adjusted to each other—how absurd that would be, at the end of the trip! More likely, we had been too busy to quarrel, and too worried abut crevasses and river crossings to worry about each other.

After our lunch some of my energy seemed to return. We had decided not to push hard that day, but to camp early, eat in relaxation, and save the hard push for what we hoped would be the last day. After that, if necessary, we could go without food for a day or two. The only thing that could stop us was a river off the map. We were already nearing the lower corner of our map. From there, Don thought the road could not be more than fifteen miles distant.

We crossed three more little streams, scarcely getting our feet wet. On a game trail a little farther on, we saw our first moose: a cow and a calf. They looked us over calmly, and we carefully stayed out of their way.

The rain started falling, lightly at first. Then suddenly we were in a deluge. We put on raincoats and continued. The rain lent some variety to the going but it managed to get us wet everywhere except about the chest. We could not avoid brushing through the soaked grass and bushes.

After the rain stopped, we found the mosquitoes had almost totally disappeared. It was the happiest event since we had got across the big river. At the fourth of the little streams, the end of the terrain marked on our map, we stopped to camp. In a tiny clearing among the dwarf spruce trees we pitched the tent. This time we had a clear nearby stream, dry wood for a fire, and no mosquitoes. For the first time that day we did work that seemed a pleasure. By contrast with the grueling hiking, camping was pure delight: evenings were our favorite part of the day, and we tried to stretch them out as long as we could.

We cooked on the stove as we sat around the fire. The food seemed inadequate, as usual, but every mouthful was a tiny feast. As it grew dark, we built the fire higher; the flames held our eyes for hours, and we managed to dry all our clothes on the surrounding bushes. Don and I sat on the same side of the fire, away from the smoke. We talked aimlessly, neither about getting out nor about Deborah. I felt sad, in a way I scarcely had during the whole expedition. For once, Don and I felt close and congenial. I thought with admiration how little he had complained about the cuts, even though it looked as if they were starting to infect and still caused him enough pain to require pills at night. I thought, also, how little his injuries had slowed him down: if anything, in the last few days, I had been the one who had had trouble keeping up the pace. The night seemed suspended around us; for a few miraculous moments we talked about other mountains, about coming back next year, almost in the same spirit as we had before we even knew about Deborah.

Before getting into the tent, I walked down to the

stream for a last drink. It was the darkest night yet; the blackness gave me a feeling of malaise, and I was inordinately glad of the fire behind me, up on the little hill. There were a few stars visible among the clouds; in the north, a red bank of clouds hovered above the horizon. I saw a sharp, single mountain silhouetted in black under the clouds; caught by surprise, I realized it was Deborah. With the surprise came a burst of sadness, of longing to be back in the snow and wind. But that passed, and I walked back up to the fire, grateful again to be camped in comfort and safety.

Inside the tent it was almost pitch black. We fell asleep in the middle of a murmured conversation.

After a deep, healing sleep, we woke to the soft morning light. We felt much better and ate our last breakfast quickly, in order to get moving. The weather was clear again; we were off by 9:00 A.M.

Somewhere ahead of us we knew we should run into the gold-mining ghost town of Denali. From there it could not be more than ten miles to the road, and perhaps as few as five. But there was still no sign of man anywhere about us; for all we could tell, this dreary sidehill had never echoed to a human step or voice before that day. Three miles ahead of us we could glimpse the final corner of the long slope we had been three days in crossing; from there, perhaps, we would see Denali, or see that we still had far to go. We resolved to resist the first half of lunch until we got to the corner.

The willows were thicker than ever. Sometimes, to

get through them, we were reduced to crawling on our hands and knees, like animals through a cane brake. We saw dozens of moose and discovered that, for all their size, they found it much easier than we did to get through the thickets. On the other hand, the moose didn't have to carry seventy-pound packs.

At one point Don looked down to the broad, silver Susitna River below us and caught sight of a bull moose swimming easily across it. Although we were getting tired and irritable again, we stood watching for a long moment, awed by the beast's power and grace.

Don's boots, saturated with water, were beginning to lose their shape. The right boot especially was failing to give him support. Walking on the continual slope, he was slowly spraining his right ankle. It began to grow very painful, but there was nothing we could do about it.

A mile before the corner, we stopped to rest. As we were sitting, looking down again at the river, I suddenly noticed a half-collapsed cabin on its bank. We were tempted to hike down to it, on the chance that an old trail might lead away from it. But there was too great a likelihood that it had been approached only by boat, from the river. Still, the sight encouraged us about the possible nearness of Denali.

At noon we reached the corner. I hurried ahead to look around the edge. At first I could see nothing but grass and brush, the same as we had crossed for the previous two days. Then suddenly, about a mile off, I spotted a shiny object, apparently the metal roof of a cabin. I yelled to Don, who brought the binoculars. Through them we could see the building itself, and several others clustered around it. It must be Denali!

After our half-lunch, the mile passed quickly. In my enthusiasm I almost doubled my pace, but Don's ankle was seriously sore, and I had to keep waiting for him. At 1:00 P.M. we reached the first of the buildings, a wreck of a shaft with the dim legend "Ladybird Mining Co." still visible on it. We ate the rest of our last lunch on the spot. Almost symbolically, Don's watch stopped as we sat there and would not start again.

A little shower urged us on. We followed an old rut of a road into the main part of the ghost town; but it took most of an hour to get there, for we had to wind deviously down, almost to the Susitna River itself, then back up a hill, crossing a medium-sized stream on the way. Though we had to wade above our knees, we didn't even bother taking off our pants or boots.

We rested for a long while on the porch of the main cabin, which looked recently rebuilt. It was also apparent that a tractor trail led off through the woods toward the road. There could be no more obstacles, then: we had made it. As the sun set, we tried to dry off in its last, warm rays. We cooked our final meal and ate in leisurely silence, trying to make the food last as long as we could.

There was nothing left to do but to hike down the tractor trail to the road. We should be able to make good time; even if it were ten miles long, we might cover it that night. It seemed to me that we should have felt more excited than we did. There was a tinge of excitement, to be sure, but it was absorbed in a dull sense of loss. And there was something else—a hint of foreboding connected with all the thoughts we had nourished in the last weeks, the thoughts of food, of ease, of company and conversation.

As the twilight deepened toward night, we started off. The trail was easy to follow and consequently monotonous. For about a mile we kept up a good pace, without a rest. But in the absence of suspense about our goal, a dozen physical irritations began to show up: the beginnings of new blisters on our feet, our aching shoulders, sores around the hips from the waist loop, the scratch of wet flannel on the crotch. Soon it was genuinely dark: we could barely make out the trail and the enclosing columns of trees. We crossed half a dozen little streams, wading them without caring about getting wet.

We had been going more than twelve hours; all at once both of us felt very tired. We rested several times each mile. After every rest we would slowly get to our feet, jerk our packs up, and set off again.

Three hours later there was no sign of the main road. It was too dark to guess where we were. We were so tired that we seemed to be stumbling along in a dream. We took another rest; I suggested to Don that we stop to camp. It would mean going longer without food, but we agreed we could make the last few miles more easily in the morning, after a sleep.

We went ahead a little way to look for dry ground

on which to pitch the tent. All the tundra around us was soaked. A dim, light-colored shelf ahead of us looked better, so we aimed for that. As we got near, the shelf seemed to stretch in either direction. Then we saw that it was the road.

We took one more, giddy rest, then hiked up the road. It was only a mile to the Susitna Lodge. We came over a rise near it and saw its light ahead. Within minutes we were turning in the driveway. The place seemed deserted. It was the darkest part of the night, probably after midnight. We remembered the lodge from the first day, when its owner had driven us out to our starting point. Now we had come full circle.

We climbed the steps and tried the front door; it was open. In the kitchen, a light was on. We looked in; a girl saw us and gave a frightened gasp. We calmed her, told her she was the first person we had seen in forty-two days, and asked if she could give us something to eat.

Nervously, she cooked us cheeseburgers and served us blueberry pie. As we devoured the food, the girl looked at us in silent fright. She seemed most upset by the sight of the lower part of Don's face. We asked if the owner was up; no, she said, everyone else was asleep. We were still hungry after the food, but the girl obviously wanted to go to bed. We could wait till morning.

In the parking lot we set up our rain fly again, as we had on the first day of the trip, and crawled into our sleeping bags beneath it. An electric light glared over us like a watchman, and a generator roared noisily from a power shed beside the driveway. It looked as if it might rain again. I asked Don how his feet were. He said that they felt all right. In his single, short answer I heard all the vague sorrow that was also building in me. Don fell asleep just as it began to rain lightly. I lay there, on the verge of sleep, thinking of ice-cream cones and baseball games and the wonderful ease, the ease of walking on sidewalks and of driving cars, the luxury of soft chairs and indoor fires, and especially the ease of unanxious sleep. But sixty miles north of us, already touched with winter snows, Deborah lay fathomless in the darkness, and nothing would ever be easy again.

Postlude ▲

In the summer of 1967, Don returned to the east ridge of Deborah with four other outstanding climbers, making up one of the strongest parties ever to climb in Alaska. They hoped to conserve time by flying in to the West Fork Glacier, climbing quickly to the col where Don and I had spent our twenty days, and receiving an airdrop there so that they could make a sustained siege on the route.

That summer I was involved in another expedition in Alaska, two hundred and fifty miles southwest of Deborah. I felt a pang of regret not to be with Don and the others but it was balanced by my fear of Deborah. Don and I had not seen each other since the Christmas of 1965, but our occasional letters had grown longer and, in the last months before we set off separately for Alaska, more intimate again. Don, too, seemed to have mixed feelings about going back to Deborah. In one letter he confided "In wakefulness it sometimes looks like a jolly good climb . . . but in the subconscious it has always been cruel."

In the middle of the expedition I was on, when our pilot flew in with supplies, we heard the news that Don's expedition had failed. They had reached the col almost immediately; but after twenty-five days of storm, including an earthquake, days in which their tents were often buried in drifting snow, they had managed to reach a point only about a hundred feet higher than the snow plume from which Don and I had turned back in 1964. Don himself had been sick for most of the trip (his illness was later diagnosed as bronchitis) and had not climbed at all above the col.

When I heard about their failure, I felt a shock of disappointment of my own; when I learned that Don had been sick, I felt closer to him than I had for a long time: it was so unfair to him, to the months (actually years, I realized) of ambivalent commitment to "the black heart of that monster," as he had called it in his letter.

Yet I felt also a sense of relief, almost an exhilaration. I tried to tell myself that it was relief that at least Don was all right—that nothing more serious than failure had happened to their expedition. But I knew it was partly relief that they had failed, that the mountain's upper ridge still loomed as formidable as only unknown places can be, and that this strong party's tiny improvement on Don's and my previous effort had thereby vindicated ours. But I had not wanted Don to fail—my pride would have been a small price to pay for his success. After a little while, I was struck by the resemblance of these feelings to the mixed ones we had felt about each other in 1964: perhaps that explained why I then felt closer to Don and, at the same time, further than ever from him.

As of 1970, Deborah's east ridge remains unclimbed. No party at present, so far as I know, has any plans to attempt it.